P9-DER-524

Contents

Responsive Classroom®

How to Bullyproof Your Classroom

Caltha Crowe

NORTHEAST FOUNDATION FOR CHILDREN, INC.

All net proceeds from the sale of this book support the work of Northeast Foundation for Children, Inc. (NEFC). NEFC, a not-for-profit educational organization, is the developer of the *Responsive Classroom*® approach to teaching, which fosters safe, challenging, and joyful elementary classrooms and schools.

The stories in this book are all based on real events in the classroom. However, in order to respect the privacy of students, names and many identifying characteristics of students and situations have been changed.

ISBN: 978-1-892989-49-9

Library of Congress Control Number: 2012934332

Cover and book design by Helen Merena.
Photographs © Alice Proujansky, Jeff Woodward, and Peter Wrenn. All rights reserved.

We would like to thank the teachers and students who so graciously welcomed Northeast Foundation for Children to take pictures in their classroom.

Northeast Foundation for Children, Inc.
85 Avenue A, Suite 204
P.O. Box 718
Turners Falls, MA 01376-0718

800-360-6332
www.responsiveclassroom.org

Printed on recycled paper

What Is Bullying?
What Can Classroom Teachers
Do About It?

• • •

His mom snapped photos as Paul climbed up the high steps onto the school bus for his first ride to school. Paul stepped into the aisle and headed toward the back. But as he walked down the aisle, looking for a seat, he tripped and sprawled onto the floor. His lunch box snapped open and yogurt from his lunch smeared on the bus flooring and down the front of his new shirt. He found an empty seat and sat, looking determinedly down at his lap, tears streaming down his face. Next to him, Sam, the only other kindergartner on the bus, whispered, "Cry baby." Paul continued to look down.

Paul's first bus ride to school set a pattern of abuse from Sam. When kids their age rode the bus, Sam told them not to sit with Paul. Sometimes he snatched away Paul's jacket or hat. Soon, other kids joined in with the bullying. They laughed, grabbed Paul's hat and passed it around the bus. This mean behavior continued, daily, for the next eight years, escalating from name calling to poking, pinching, shoving, and tripping.

Paul was a different child at home than he was at school. At home Paul loved to bike ride, go fishing with his dad, watch movies with the family, or trade jokes with his mom. At school, his teachers noticed that he didn't socialize with the other children. As Paul got older, he did his homework each night. But when parent-teacher conference time rolled around, his teacher reported that Paul often didn't turn in his homework.

Despite regular home-school communication, the problem persisted. Because he was too sad and fearful to remember his homework or pay attention in class, Paul's academic progress was sporadic. His parents talked with him about why he was having such a hard time with school, but Paul never said anything about the bullying. Though the bullying was persistent and deeply distressing, Paul, like many children who are targeted for bullying, was too ashamed and afraid to tell an adult.

In middle school, Paul finally confided in a trusted guidance counselor. The guidance counselor confronted Paul's tormentors. In time, Paul healed from the years of bullying—he made friends, enrolled in martial arts, and took on a leadership role.

Not all children recover so well. News reports recount too many stories of children who commit violent acts against themselves or others in response to persistent bullying.

Paul's story is played out every day in schools around the world. A child, like Sam, picks on another child, engaging in behaviors like name-calling and other mistreatments. Adults are unaware of the mean behavior and therefore do not intervene. When adults do not step in, children assume that the behavior is OK and the meanness escalates, with class-mates encouraging the mean behavior through watching, laughing, and even joining in. After many years of being treated in this way, adolescents often can't imagine that their life will ever improve.

Children's lives in school don't need to be this way. Teachers in many schools and classrooms teach children how to be kind and inclusive. In these classrooms there are clear rules about how to treat one another, les-sons to help children recognize bullying and other mean behavior, and protocols to help them befriend children who are targeted and report the mean behavior to responsible adults.

The focus of this book is on preventing bullying—by identifying and intervening in the small, mean behaviors that can escalate into full-blown bullying and by creating an environment where kindness rather than meanness prevails.

What Is Bullying?

I begin by defining bullying for the simple reason that this is a book about preventing it. But there's a perhaps less obvious reason for teachers to understand how bullying differs from other kinds of mean behavior: For the safety of the targeted child, bullying requires a different set of responses from adults than aggression that grows out of conflict between equals. I talk about this in the chapters that follow.

For the purposes of this book, I define "bullying" as behavior by a person or group that establishes, asserts, or maintains social power over another person and causes pain or humiliation. Sometimes bullying is long-term and debilitating, as in Paul's case; sometimes it begins and ends within a span of weeks. Even a one-time act, however, can be mean and used to establish, assert, or maintain dominance.

[handwritten margin note: It's not between "equal" powered individuals]

There are many variations in how people define bullying. At the time of this writing, most states in the United States have laws designed to protect children against bullying in school. Each of these states has a slightly different definition of bullying, and behavior I describe as bullying may or may not refer to behavior that is a reportable offense in your state. To understand when and how to officially report bullying, you will need to become familiar with your state's guidelines. In addition, many of the researchers I refer to in the following pages use definitions of bullying that differ slightly from each other.

[handwritten margin note: • direct & indirect]

[handwritten margin note: ★ bullying is about social power]

However, all the definitions have in common the idea that bullying is one-sided, that there is an imbalance of power, and that the bullying behavior hurts and humiliates the person who is targeted.

Bullying can be physical, relational, or both

Bullying can consist of an act or series of acts of physical violence, such as hitting, pinching, tripping, spilling things on someone, or shoving. Bullying can also consist of acts of relational aggression such as purposely excluding someone or spreading rumors about someone.

Relational bullying can be direct or indirect. When Matt says to the other children in his class, "Let's call Mia 'Fluffernutter,'" and they chant "Fluffernutter, Fluffernutter" softly in the cafeteria, so that Mia can hear while the adults can't, that's direct relational aggression. If Matt had told everyone, "Don't play with Mia," and Mia couldn't figure out why no one would play with her, that's indirect relational aggression. I would call both acts bullying because both are assertions of power by Matt over Mia and both cause her pain and humiliation.

Scope of the problem

Bullying is pervasive and worldwide, not rooted in any one culture. Children bully other children in rural, urban, and suburban schools, at every income level. Dr. Dan Olweus, the Scandinavian psychologist who originated modern bullying prevention programs, reported in 2010 on data gathered from a sample of 524,000 elementary and high school children in the United States who responded to the Olweus Bullying Questionnaire (Olweus & Limber, 2010). In the questionnaire, bullying is defined, in child-friendly terms, as negative, hurtful behavior that occurred repeatedly and involved an imbalance of power. Questions are multiple choice and the responses use specific language that is designed to minimize subjective reporting. For example, a question might ask if a particular behavior occurred once a month, two or three times a week, etc., rather than using terms such as "seldom" or "frequently." Questions cover a range of bullying behaviors that fall into three general categories: direct bullying, such as physical aggression or name-calling; indirect bullying, such as exclusion or rumor spreading; and cyberbullying.

Data showed that for children in grades three to five, 20%–25% of the children reported being targeted for bullying behavior at least two to three times in the previous month. Nearly 10% of the elementary school children in the database admitted to bullying others in the past month (Olweus & Limber, 2010). Other researchers report that as many as 33.7% of elementary school children in the United States say that they have been bullied at some time (Bradshaw, Sawyer, & O'Brennan, 2007).

Bullying behavior frequently starts as early as preschool or kindergarten as children begin to establish power relationships (Alsaker, n.d.; Pellegrini et al., 2007). Multiple studies have demonstrated that many children continue to be targeted year after year. Dan Olweus reports that 39% of elementary school girls and 45% of elementary school boys who reported being bullied said that they had been bullied for more than a year. Fifty percent of the high school students who reported being bullied had been bullied for more than a year (Olweus & Limber, 2010).

Who is part of a bullying interaction?

The child doing the bullying

Bullying is about power—gaining power, asserting it, and maintaining it. It's difficult—and not very useful—to assign a "bully personality profile." In the past, bullies were often described as the child who was an outcast, on the fringes. In contrast to that, some studies have shown that children who bully repeatedly are often the popular kids, with high self-esteem (Menesini et al., 2003). One recent study shows that students who engage in bullying behavior are often in the middle of the social hierarchy and use bullying as a way to achieve higher status (Faris & Felmlee, 2011).

The common characteristic is that the child who bullies sees assertion of power as desirable and social/emotional or physical aggression as the best—or only—way to rise in the social hierarchy.

The study done in 2003 by Menesini et al. also showed that children who repeatedly bully show moral disengagement and lack of empathy. They often think that what they're doing is just fine and it's the targeted child's own fault that he or she is different and thus deserving of being treated meanly. They feel that they deserve power and that "the loser" deserves the treatment he or she is receiving.

The child who is targeted

Although all children have the potential to be targeted for bullying, some are more frequently targeted. Children who are shy or less assertive

Use Language That Focuses on the Action, Not the Person

Everyone has the potential to engage in mean behaviors. For most, it's a transient action. But some people can get stuck in the mean behavior. When we use terms like "the bully" we risk stereotyping children and helping them stay stuck in that role. For that reason, throughout this book I use phrases that focus on the action rather than the person—for example, "bullying behavior" and "the person doing the bullying." These phrases communicate a belief that the person can do better and open the door for change.

Similarly, terms like "the victim" risk stereotyping a bullied child as weak or helpless. It's only a few steps from calling someone "the victim" to blaming them for playing that role. If instead we refer to the "person who is targeted," we place responsibility on the person doing the bullying and free from blame the person who is targeted.

than others have few strategies for protecting themselves. Children who are different in any number of ways may be targeted especially frequently. Jo Ann Freiberg, the Connecticut State Department of Education bullying consultant, reports that her caseload of children being targeted overwhelmingly consists of children with special needs (J. Freiberg, personal communication, June 2010). Looking different, acting different, or having self-protection skills that are less developed than those of their classmates all make the children in her caseload more likely to be targeted.

Children who do not conform to gender stereotypes can also be targeted. "She plays with the boys" or "He's gay" might be the opening gambits (Felix & Green, 2010). Children who are overweight, children who dress differently, children whose family incomes are different, either lower or higher, from those of their classmates, or children whose skills and interests are simply different from those of their classmates may be targeted (Gordon, 2010; Olweus et al., 2007).

Studies show that among the characters in this drama are a small number of children who go back and forth, sometimes instigating mean behavior and sometimes being the children who are targeted for mean behavior (Olweus, 1993). These are often the children who have poor social skills, are quick to anger, lack self-control, and have few or no friends to support them. Marie, who is often picked on or ignored, discovers that if she spreads gossip about Kaitlyn she's suddenly the center of attention in the classroom. However, next week Marie may be targeted when Kaitlyn rallies friends to gang up on her.

Witnesses to the mean behavior

Bullying is a social act. Researchers have found that 85% of bullying incidents include not just the child who bullies and the child targeted but also an audience: the children who witness the mean behavior. These bystanders are an important part of the equation. Often, the child who bullies will be trying to appear powerful to the audience as much as to the child targeted. In many cases, bullying needs this audience if it is to thrive; one way to thwart the bullying is for the audience to show disapproval (Craig & Pepler, 1998).

The Olweus Bullying Prevention Program describes multiple roles that bystanders might play. At one end are those who actively join in the bullying. At the other end are those who try to help the child who is targeted. Most bystanders fall in between. Some don't take an active part but support the bullying through laughter or other signs of approval; others simply watch. Some quiet bystanders might be uncomfortable with the bullying behavior, but they don't intervene (Olweus et al., 2007).

Even if bystanders only watch, the message to the child doing the bullying is that his or her behavior is acceptable. On the other hand, if bystanders show disapproval, the message is quite the opposite and can have a powerful effect. In a classic Canadian study, researchers used hidden video cameras and microphones to observe children on the playground. They found that 57% of the time when peers intervened in bullying incidents the mean behavior stopped in an average of ten seconds (Craig & Pepler, 1998).

All too often, bullying prevention policies focus on how to teach the children who are targeted to stand up to bullying. This is not a realistic approach. We don't expect people who are robbed at gunpoint to stand up to the criminals. We don't expect people who are targets of domestic abuse to "just walk away" or to "tell the batterer to stop." We need to make bullying as socially unacceptable as domestic abuse or armed robbery. We need to teach children to take care of each other—we need to turn bystanders into allies.

Adults

Adults are often unaware of bullying behavior in schools and classrooms. In study after study, the adults underestimated the prevalence of bullying. In the Canadian study mentioned above (Craig & Pepler, 1998), researchers observed behavior on the playground and in classrooms. They recorded an average of one bullying incident every seven minutes. Adults intervened in only 4% of these incidents. Even more amazing is the fact that when they observed classrooms, researchers noted that adults intervened in only 14% of the incidents that happened when the adults were present in the room, despite the fact that 71% of these same adults reported that they "nearly always" intervened in bullying incidents.

In Dan Olweus's 2010 report of the attitudes of more than half a million school children, 60% said that over the past two months bullying incidents had happened in their classroom with a teacher present but not intervening. The slight bright spot here is that the figure drops to 50% if we look at just the younger children in the sample, the third through fifth graders. The other 50% of the third through fifth graders said that their teachers sometimes "tried to stop the bullying" (Olweus & Limber, 2010).

What Can We Do?

A wealth of research as well as the experiences of classroom teachers tells us that there's a lot that teachers can do to prevent bullying in their classrooms and in their schools (Bear, 1998; Bullock, 2002; Kasen, Berenson, Cohen, & Johnson, 2004; Katz & Chard, 2000; Pepler & Craig, 2007).

- First, teachers can build a classroom community where everyone feels valued and included. They can help students build strong, positive relationships with each other and with the teacher and they can establish rules that guide children toward kind, friendly, inclusive behavior.

■ Once the rules are established, teachers can take the time to help children understand how the rules apply to a range of school situations and make sure children know that teachers hold them accountable for their behavior.

■ Teachers can also increase their observation and awareness of the small, mean behaviors that can develop into bullying.

■ Finally, teachers can give students the tools they'll need to address mean behavior when they witness it.

Taking these steps will decrease the likelihood of unkind behavior and increase the likelihood that students will stand up for each other and report unkind behavior to the teacher.

Much current research and writing focuses on schoolwide practices to address bullying. And indeed, a schoolwide approach is optimal. But even if your school has not instituted schoolwide changes, you can do much in your classroom and in collaboration with grade-level team members to create a safe climate for learning.

My experience, over thirty-plus years in elementary schools, is that children can meet the expectations of the classroom, even when those expectations are quite different from those outside the classroom. Moreover, children can take what they learn in the classroom out into the wider world around them. As you change your classroom, you might just be taking steps toward changing your school.

Strategies to Prevent Bullying

In writing this book, I drew on my many years of experience as a classroom teacher as well as on the wealth of thinking and research on how to prevent bullying. For much of my teaching career, I used the *Responsive Classroom*® approach to teaching. One of its missions is to give teachers the tools they need to create and maintain safe, caring, and joyful classrooms and to teach children to be kind and caring outside the classroom walls as well.

Many of the strategies of the approach are effective strategies for bullying prevention. In the following chapters you'll find information about helping children get to know each other through the structures of a daily Morning Meeting, creating positively stated rules that are connected to students' learning goals, using Interactive Modeling and role-playing to help children apply expectations to specific situations, and responding quickly and calmly to misbehavior.

If you are already familiar with the *Responsive Classroom* approach, I hope you'll gain a new appreciation of how consistent use of *Responsive Classroom* strategies can be an effective tool in your bullying prevention efforts. And if you are not implementing the *Responsive Classroom* approach, I believe you can find ways to adapt these strategies to your own classroom structures. If you'd like to learn more about the approach, you'll find rich resources at www.responsiveclassroom.org.

Topics covered in this book include the following:

Addressing gateway behaviors. I begin the book by talking about gateway behaviors—those small acts of disrespect or unkindness that we often let slide, giving children the message that these behaviors are acceptable (Englander & Schank, 2010). We hear one child call another child names. We notice two children sitting close together in a way that excludes another child. We hear about one child taking another child's cookie at lunch.

Although these are small acts, lack of attention to such behaviors can lead to full-blown bullying. It's important to notice and respond to these behaviors appropriately, nonpunitively, and calmly. Keeping the response nonpunitive is especially important—there is research that shows that when children are exposed to aggressive punishments, they become more aggressive (Kaufman, 1994).

The goal is to firmly show children that meanness is unacceptable, to teach them more appropriate social skills, and to help them begin to develop habits of kindness. To learn more about this, see Chapter One.

Building a positive and safe classroom community from day one. Research indicates that bullying happens less frequently in classrooms where all children are included in activities (Gottfredson, 2001; Greene, 2006; Newman, Murray, & Lussier, 2001). It also indicates that bullying happens less frequently in classrooms where the teacher shows warmth and responsiveness to children (Olweus, Limber, & Mihalic, 2000). Researchers have discovered that these variables account for widely divergent amounts of bullying behavior in the same school and even among various classes at the same grade level (Henry et al., 2000). I'll present a number of strategies in Chapters Two, Three, and Four that will help you create a safe classroom community.

Creating rules. Rules are essential guideposts to children's behavior and are a key ingredient in most evidence-based bullying prevention programs (Swearer, Espelage, Vaillancourt, & Hymel, 2010). Rules set the standard for how children treat each other, their classroom, and their work. But for rules to be effective, teachers need to do ongoing work with students to help them understand how the classroom rules apply to day-to-day situations. For more information about creating and applying rules, see Chapter Three.

Addressing "tattling." To effectively address bullying, we need children to become allies who protect the child targeted for bullying by reporting to an adult. But all too often we give mixed messages, on the one hand asking children to tell us about bullying and on the other hand chastising them for "tattling."

Without adequate teaching about what and how to report, children are reluctant to report bullying to responsible adults in school. Younger children are more willing to report than older children. Nonetheless, in the database of more than 500,000 responses to the Olweus Bullying Questionnaire, 70% of the third graders (the youngest children in the sample) who reported being bullied in the past two months had not told a teacher (Olweus & Limber, 2010).

This reluctance to report bullying results in the continuation of bullying behaviors because children need adult intervention to stop such behaviors. But it's also important to help children understand the difference between telling the teacher about small behaviors that they can let go of or resolve independently and reporting mean behavior to a responsible adult to keep someone safe. To learn more about this, see Chapters Three and Six.

Addressing outside-the-classroom behaviors. Research shows that a lot of bullying and pre-bullying behavior occurs in areas of the school outside of the classroom, such as the hallway, playground, lunchroom, and school bus (Olweus & Limber, 2010). Schoolwide rules and anti-bullying protocols are an important piece of addressing bullying in these areas. But there's also a lot that classroom teachers can do to help children apply the kind behaviors they're learning in the classroom to other parts of the school. In Chapter Five, you'll learn about specific strategies for helping students be better school citizens.

Working with parents. Communication with parents is a critical element in preventing bullying. Parents can let teachers know about children's behavior at home that might indicate problems at school and teachers can let parents know about classroom bullying prevention strategies. One international meta-analysis of bullying prevention programs found that a strong parent component was an important part of every successful bullying prevention program (Farrington & Ttofi, 2009). You'll find information about working with parents in each chapter.

Teaching children about bullying. Children need to know what bullying is and how to prevent it. Direct teaching may help a child who is tempted to bully to stop and think. It may empower a child who is targeted to seek help. The most effective lessons about bullying,

About the Term "Parent"

Students come from a variety of homes with a variety of family structures. Students might be raised by grandparents, siblings, aunts, uncles, and foster families. I want to honor all these people for devoting their time, love, and attention to raising children. However, it's hard to find just one word that adequately encompasses all these caregivers. For simplicity's sake, I use "parent" to refer to anyone who is a child's primary caregiver.

however, focus on helping children who witness bullying to be an ally of the child who is targeted. Children can learn to avoid laughing at the targeted child's expense, to befriend that child and comfort him, and, most important, to tell a responsible adult.

To have a positive classroom and school climate free from meanness that might escalate into bullying behaviors, we also need to directly teach children some of the subtleties of social discourse. What is the difference between laughing for fun, say at a silly joke, and laughing at someone's expense, which violates our rule to be kind? Why is it important to refer to people by their names rather than unfriendly nicknames that they may not like?

For more about this, including lesson plan ideas, see Chapter Six.

[handwritten: bullying lesson plans p155]

Final Thoughts

Teachers have an important opportunity—and an obligation—to curb mean behavior. The elementary school years are a period during which adults can make a big difference. Children in grades K–5 are more willing to turn to adults for help solving relationship problems than are their older peers. Furthermore, children's attitudes toward school and learning are formed in the early years of school. By creating a climate of safety and inclusion in elementary school classrooms, teachers can support children in taking risks and discovering the joys of learning in their current lives and in the years to come.

Chapter One

Gateway Behaviors: What to Do When Mean Acts Emerge

• • •

Arriving at school in the morning, fifth graders take down their chairs as Ms. Hernandez collects homework and oversees lunch sign-up. Max approaches Jason. "Did your mom let you watch *Terminator* last night or did she make you go to bed early?" he asks. "Naw," Jason replies, a little abashed, "She told me I had to go to bed." Max looks at Jason with a smirk while Jason turns away, clearly uncomfortable. In the competition for who gets to be the most grown-up, Max is the winner because he got to stay up until midnight on a school night. Moreover, he got to watch an R-rated movie. Is Max's behavior bullying? No, of course not. But it is a first step in social competition.

Next door, as children trickle into their third grade classroom, Missy whispers to Laticia, "Your hair is nappy. You'll never get a boyfriend." Is it bullying? Maybe. We'd need to know more to be sure. Whether or not it's bullying, it's certainly social aggression.

When these small aggressive acts are unchecked, they grow to permeate a classroom and become the accepted mode of interaction. Mean acts and words become the norm. It's only a few steps from competition about who is allowed more privileges at home to openly calling Jason a "baby" and next to excluding Jason from games at recess. It's even fewer steps from directly insulting Laticia about her hair to repeatedly insulting her and organizing other girls to do the same.

Once such disrespectful behaviors are normalized, they can take on a life of their own in classrooms. Classmates watch and sometimes even laugh at the cruelty, bringing the child who initiates these behaviors attention and social cachet. This attention encourages the child behaving meanly to escalate the unkind behaviors.

Barbara Coloroso, in her book *The Bully, the Bullied, and the Bystander* (2003), paints a picture of a typical bullying scenario. Children are playing on the playground. The child who is going to bully brushes up against another child as if by accident. When no one comes to the targeted child's defense, the child who is bullying snatches his classmate's ball and throws it away. If no one objects, the behaviors escalate first into name-calling, then into shoving, hitting, and more.

Stephen Wessler, in his book *The Respectful School* (2003), tells stories of children who are first insulted behind their backs. When no one objects, classmates begin to insult them to their face. When no one stops the direct insults, classmates begin to push and shove the child. When no one stops the pushing and shoving, the actions escalate into dangerous violence.

"We Need to Focus on the Small Stuff"

If we catch the small initial behaviors, referred to as "gateway behaviors" by Elizabeth Englander of the Massachusetts Aggression Reduction Center (MARC), and nip them in the bud, they won't have an opportunity to grow and blossom into out-and-out bullying. As Englander says, "We need to focus on the small stuff." The first step in meeting this challenge is to notice the small and subtle acts of aggression that may be going on in classrooms (Englander & Schank, 2010).

In the two examples cited at the beginning of this chapter, neither teacher was aware of the comments. A great deal of research demonstrates that teachers are often unaware of both small acts of social aggression—gateway behaviors to bullying—and out-and-out bullying (Craig & Pepler, 1998; Olweus & Limber, 2010). Children make comments under their breath, give a classmate a quick kick when the teacher's back is turned, or pass notes with mean comments. Amazingly, we teachers often miss these behaviors even when they happen in the classroom when we're present.

Although it's true that teachers miss many mean behaviors, it's also true that such behaviors often happen when teachers are not present, during less supervised times of the school day and in less supervised places. Children surrounding someone in a less supervised area of the playground, mocking someone on social networking sites in ways that then affect that child's feelings while at school, and picking on younger children on the school bus are all-too-common occurrences that hurt children deeply and often go undetected by adults.

School, however, doesn't need to be this way. In this chapter I describe some strategies that you can use to hone your skills of noticing mean behaviors. I discuss how to tell the difference between developmentally appropriate behaviors and gateways to bullying. Finally, I provide some guidelines for stopping the gateway behaviors.

Observe Students' Interactions

If teachers are to reduce or prevent bullying, they first need to notice the many small, mean-spirited acts that can lead to bullying. Making time for this noticing might seem daunting in a day already packed with responsibilities. Nonetheless, by making small adjustments to daily routines, you can find time for quick observations. Here are some ideas:

- **Use arrival time to observe students' interactions.** It's tempting to use arrival time for catching up on paperwork or to do administrative tasks such as lunch count and homework check-off. However, you can give students responsibility for tasks such as these. If you also put aside your other paperwork and spend time observing, you'll gain valuable information about students. With such an arrangement, Max and

Jason's teacher might have noticed their arrival time interactions. Missy and Laticia's teacher might have heard their whispered conversation.

■ **Get to the lunchroom a couple of minutes before it's time to pick up the students.** Use this time to quietly observe and learn about what the students are doing at lunchtime. I arrived at the lunchroom a few minutes early one day, just in time to hear Joey say to Michael, "Look at your ugly pasta." Bullying? No, but possibly mean and hurtful words that could escalate into bullying if we don't investigate further and intervene if the situation is truly mean teasing.

■ **Use informal moments during choice time, indoor recess, or independent work time to observe the social culture of the classroom.** Notice who gravitates toward whom and who is alone. These are both indicators of the climate of inclusion and exclusion, clues that might alert you to behaviors that are potential gateways to bullying. An inclusive classroom is protective against bullying.

Assess What You're Seeing

For observation to be useful, you'll need to assess what you're seeing and hearing so you can understand what it's telling you about your classroom and guide possible interventions. Following are some key things to pay attention to.

Notice children's words

Is the tone mean and insulting?

Take the case of Joey, Michael, and the "ugly pasta" described above. Teasing can be mean and hurtful or it can be a bonding experience between close friends. Body language can give you clues. Is the joking followed by shared laughter or is only the person who made the joke laughing? Do the children lean in together or does the person joked about pull away?

Who is enjoying the joke? Who is made uncomfortable by it? Jokes about someone else's body (the nappy hair), family ("Your mother . . ."), abilities ("You read like a baby"), and food (the ugly pasta) are often meant to demean. Jokes about shared events leading to shared laughter can solidify a friendship.

In the "ugly pasta" situation, I spoke with Michael privately and asked him how he felt when Joey made the comment about his pasta. "It hurt my feelings when he made fun of my food," Michael responded. Later on I had a serious private talk with Joey. For a few weeks I kept a close eye on the two boys, looking for any signs of further mean behavior. I found, though, that the early intervention appeared to stop it.

Is code being used to indicate who is "in" and who is "out"?

Besides mean words and casual insults, no matter how small, there are more subtle things to listen for. Children's conversation reveals a lot about who is "in" and who's "out." One year the boys in my class started calling each other "Bubba." I noticed that some boys were not called "Bubba," and were left out of the "Bubba" inner circle. I followed these observations with a class discussion about nicknames. I explained that sometimes the use of nicknames can be hurtful or a means of excluding children; we agreed that in school we'd call everybody by their given name.

Notice children's interactions

Who's in charge? Who's included? Who's left out?

When students work together in small groups, whether in reading, writing, math, science, or social studies, take a minute to observe their interactions. Notice who gets a turn and who is left out, who takes charge and who sits back. These moments will give you rich information that will help you protect your classroom climate, keeping it kind and inclusive.

If someone is chronically left out, listen to conversations around that child. What are the other children saying to or about the chronically isolated child? If someone is consistently in charge, listen to the words that child uses to maintain control.

I sat quietly on the side while a group worked on a social studies project. Manuel and Sarah were planning their diorama while Justin sat and listened. Were Manuel and Sarah excluding? Was Justin sitting back and letting the others do the work? As I observed Justin over time, I noticed that no one spoke to him, and no one made a place for him in the circle, much less sought him out for work and play.

I came to discover that Justin, seemingly surrounded by classmates, was nonetheless an ignored child in the social life of the classroom. Aware of that fact because of my observations, I arranged for Justin to partner with children who might share interests with him. For reading, I partnered him with Allan, who also loved to read Danger Guys books. I noticed that Justin really enjoyed working with his kindergarten buddy and so did Miguel. I arranged for the two of them to help the kindergartners with their snowsuits at the end of the day. Soon, Miguel, Allan, and Justin were seeking one another out in the classroom. Justin was moving into the circle of our community.

Investigate why a child is isolated

Are one or more of the students in your classroom, like Justin, always alone? If there's an opportunity to choose partners, are these students the last chosen? Where is this isolation coming from? Finding answers may take a bit of investigating, including a conversation with the child who is isolated.

Be sure to check in with the child privately. My experience and that of many experts who work to prevent bullying is that children who are targeted for bullying are so intimidated that they're unlikely to be truthful in front of the children who are being unkind (Moretsky & Thomas, 2010; Parker-Roerden, Rudewick, & Gorton, 2007; StopBullying.gov, n.d.).

When I noticed that Suzy was always alone on the playground, I asked her about it in a private moment. "Clarisse doesn't like me anymore," she explained. It turned out that Clarisse had told all of the other girls not to play with Suzy. I knew I needed to act on that information.

I had a private talk with Clarisse. I told her that I'd noticed that Suzy was alone on the playground. I asked her what she'd noticed about who was included in the group of girls who played together. Her response was "Suzy's a baby; we don't like to play with her." I let her know that it wasn't OK to exclude Suzy. "Suzy's a member of our classroom community. You need to include her in games on the playground, just the way you include others," I said.

I also told her that I'd heard from a couple of sources that she had been telling others not to play with Suzy. I didn't open it up for discussion. I simply said, "Our rule says we'll be kind to all. It's not OK to tell others not to play with someone. I know that you can be kind and include everyone. I'll be watching to make sure that you do."

I helped other girls in the class connect with Suzy by arranging reading and writing partnerships. I also used some strategies with the whole class such as revisiting our rule to be kind and leading a role-play on how to include everyone. Soon Suzy was back in the mix of girls playing together on the playground.

Lastly, keep in mind that a child's sitting alone does not always indicate exclusion. For example, one day I arrived to pick up students in the lunchroom. As I stood and watched for a minute, I saw Halima sitting alone on the edge of the group. Later on I asked her, privately, about her lunchroom seat. "I like to sit there because then I can talk with Dorthea, my friend in Mrs. Kelly's class," she explained. So she wasn't being excluded; she was just making a choice.

If You Suspect Bullying, Do Not Use Conflict Resolution

In the situation involving Suzy and Clarisse, I did not use the strategy of a conflict resolution meeting. When one child tells others not to play with a classmate, this is not a conflict to be resolved between the child doing the telling and the one being excluded. It's an aggressive act that needs to be stopped. Conflict resolution meetings are a strategy used between equal participants to help them learn to listen to each other. When there's behavior that could be bullying, as in the situation with Suzy and Clarisse, it's unfair—and possibly dangerous—to the child who is targeted to expect her or him to take part in a conflict resolution meeting.

Consider children's stage of development: Is this typical behavior? Is it OK behavior?

Was the spate of "Bubba" nicknames in my classroom a developmentally predictable behavior? Perhaps. Nevertheless, it was exclusionary and thus not acceptable in our classroom any more than "clubs" were.

In contrast, some developmentally predictable behaviors may look unkind but in actuality be OK, not necessarily destructive to the classroom feeling of community. When two eleven-year-old girls pick each other out as "best friends" they're learning how to have a close friend, an important part of life. It's important to make sure that they are friendly to all their classmates and continue to work with children who are not part of the dyad, but no one would benefit from trying to prevent the selective friendship.

How do you know whether children are engaging in cruel behaviors, a step along the continuum toward bullying? How do you know how to respond? Here are some things to look for:

Look for equity

Kindergartners sometimes express displeasure by saying "You can't come to my birthday party," never mind that the birthday is six months away, in the summer, and no party is planned. Usually "You can't come to my birthday party" is said after a tablemate snatches a crayon or takes someone's place in line. It's one way that a five-year-old knows to express displeasure.

If the "You can't come to my birthday party" insult is equally expressed, back and forth between two children, then it's probably not a step along the bullying continuum, although it does call for some social skills instruction on what to do if someone snatches your crayon or cuts in front of you in line.

On the other hand, if there's one child who consistently is told that he's not coming to anyone's birthday party, consistently told that he can play only if he'll be the dog, then there's a power imbalance that might very well grow into bullying.

Look at children's facial expressions and body language

Watch to see whether children's expressions are friendly, neutral, or grudging. Look at their bodies. Do they lean into their partner or away? Is their posture open and welcoming or closed?

Many eleven-year-old boys love to trade insults. If two boys are engaged in such a contest, and each is giving as good as he gets, the situation has met the standard of equity. If they're both laughing and smiling, they're probably engaged in verbal play rather than taking a step down the path toward bullying.

The six-year-old boys' equivalent to older boys' trading of insults is rough-and-tumble play. As the first graders burst onto the playground after a morning of concentrated academic work, they butt and roll like puppies. This may or may not be allowed in your school. But it's most likely not an expression of social aggression unless there's one boy who's getting knocked over all the time and others who are doing all the knocking. Are they all laughing and smiling or is there one who doesn't look like he's enjoying this type of play?

Pay attention to children who might be at risk of being targeted

Anyone has the potential to be targeted by bullying behavior. Nonetheless, some children are more likely to be targeted than others.

Consider Choosing Safety

It can be difficult to tell whether seemingly mean words are hurtful or not, first steps toward bullying or bonding events between equals. In the end, you may decide, for the sake of emotional and physical safety, to simply tell students, "We only use kind words in this class." Children can trade insults in fun at home.

You may also decide to simply say, "In this class we keep our bodies to ourselves." Rough-and-tumble play can be reserved for situations outside of school. You may decide to say, "In this class, everyone needs someone to play with, so we include everyone unless they want to be by themselves."

Such guidelines will clarify for children what is—and is not—acceptable behavior and will minimize the number of judgment calls you need to make in assessing children's interactions.

Children who don't conform to gender stereotypes

For example, the girl who prefers to play football or the boy who likes to play with dolls are at risk for bullying (Felix & Green, 2010). Keep your eyes open to see if such children are being excluded, surreptitiously insulted, or nudged out of the way.

Children receiving special education services

Many researchers identify children receiving special education services as being at risk for bullying because they may seem a bit different to their classmates (Freiberg, 2009; Olweus & Limber, 2007; StopBullying.gov, n.d.). It's important to make sure that children receiving special education services are included and treated respectfully.

Children from a different economic level

Income disparity is another risk factor for bullying. The child whose family income is either higher or lower than that of other families so that her clothing and other belongings aren't quite like those of classmates may be targeted for teasing and exclusion (Harachi et al., 2006; Swearer, 2010).

When I began teaching, one of my colleagues told me that I'd need to have "eyes in the back of the head." Those eyes need to be wide open to protect the at-risk child.

Pay attention to children who might be at risk of engaging in bullying behavior

Anyone has the potential to engage in meanness and bullying behavior. Nonetheless, there are some risk factors governing who may fall into that role as well.

The child in the middle

If bullying is about gaining and maintaining social power, then it's important to watch those children in the middle of the social hierarchy who might be trying to gain power as well as those children who have gained power through sometimes subtle cruelty and are seeking to maintain it.

The "popular" child

Research done in the last ten years has shown that popular kids, as well as children in the middle striving for popularity, are often the children who bully (Menesini et al., 2003).

Often those "popular" children are liked by adults as well as by other children. It's easy to miss the fact that someone who's so likeable is being cruel. The popular child may be articulate, funny, physically attractive, and good at sports and have lots of friends. These qualities may be as attractive to adults as they are to children.

It's important to observe students' behavior objectively, paying attention to the child whom you like so much that you may be inadvertently making too many allowances for her or his unkind behavior.

Mrs. Sharpe is a school librarian in a small rural school. She sees all students in the school once a week for library class and thus knows every student well. "There's a boy in sixth grade that everyone picks on," she told me. "The children take off their shoes when they sit on the library carpet," she continues. "They're all sitting there and suddenly they start to say, 'Eww, Jackson's feet smell.' Well, all of their feet smell, but they're all blaming Jackson."

I asked her if someone started the insults and she said that she'd watch and see. A few weeks later she told me, "I've been noticing. It's always Wayne who starts it off. Once he starts in on Jackson, the others follow. They all want to be Wayne's friend. I don't blame them. I'd like to be Wayne's friend, too. He's smart, he's funny, and he's good at sports."

It's important to notice children who might be at risk. It's also important not to make assumptions. Any child can be targeted. Any child can find himself sucked into behaving aggressively. If you watch objectively, you'll be positioned to be most helpful to all students.

Intervening: Stop Small Behaviors Before They Become Big Problems

Once you've done some observing so that you understand students' social interactions, the next step is to use that understanding to stop behaviors that might be gateways to bullying when it's still relatively easy to do so. Sometimes teachers are unsure whether they should step in when someone says "Your pasta is ugly." Isn't he just expressing his opinion? Well, yes, but he's also possibly being unkind. What about, "Your hair is nappy and you'll never get a boyfriend"? That's certainly an unkind statement about something that's very much a part of the targeted child's body—her hair. It is also a potential opening move in a chain of escalating events and is very much worth stopping.

In the following pages I'll spell out some strategies for stopping such small mean behaviors. Classroom and school rules, teacher language, fair and respectful consequences, and teacher modeling all play a part.

Stop gateway behaviors quickly

It's important to intervene as soon as you see unkind actions or hear unkind words. Elizabeth Englander of the Massachusetts Aggression Reduction Center (MARC) promotes the "nine second" rule of thumb. Spend the first two seconds noticing, she says, and then the next seven seconds briefly and firmly responding (Englander, 2011).

Although it may take you more than two seconds to figure out what's going on when one student rolls his or her eyes or makes a mean joke at the expense of another, Ms. Englander's point—that a quick response is important—fits with my experience working with children. A quick response shows the child behaving meanly, the child targeted, and those nearby that mean behavior and exclusion are unacceptable in the classroom.

In research conducted by MARC, students reported that the most damaging thing that adults did in response to gateway behaviors was to ignore them (Englander, 2011).

When adults miss the opportunity to respond quickly, they often end up looking as if they're ignoring the behavior. Bystanders then think that the behavior is acceptable, and children who say or do unkind things don't have an opportunity to learn about the impact of their behavior and how to change the behavior. In some cases, even the children targeted begin to believe that they somehow deserve the treatment that they're getting. Conditions are set for mean behaviors to flourish.

Refer to classroom rules

One of the challenges is that it's not always clear what to say and how to stop these gateway behaviors. This is where classroom rules play an important role. In Chapter Three, you'll learn about a process for establishing classroom rules that children connect to and believe in. If children are invested in the rules and understand that the rules can help keep everyone safe, the rules can provide a solid framework for stopping small cruelties.

"Our rules say to be kind; that statement was not kind," is a short and simple way to refer to the rules and stop the behavior. Another approach is to give the student the responsibility for thinking about the behavior. A teacher might ask the student to reflect by saying, "Think about our rule to be kind. How can you be kind right now?"

Whichever of these approaches you use, you are avoiding a power struggle with the student by referring to the rules. It's the rules that are saying to stop the mean behavior, not the teacher.

Use brief, matter-of-fact language to remind and redirect

Short, simple statements are most effective in stopping small unkind comments or actions. "Stop; that was not a kind statement; rewind and say it kindly," is clear and succinct. It's tempting to go on and on, telling children about all of the ramifications of their actions. You can be sure that as you go on and on they will tune you out.

A matter-of-fact tone will allow children to listen. In contrast, a blaming or shaming tone will lead children to feel belittled and resentful. The same words can sound calm or shrill, straightforward or sarcastic. Statements such as "That sounds unkind," or "Keep your feet in your own personal space," will be heard best if they're stated calmly.

Try coming up with some potential statements that you might use when you hear unkind comments or see unkind actions. Practice them. That way, in the actual situation, you'll have some phrases and a matter-of-fact tone of voice that will come naturally.

For more information about reminding and redirecting language, see *The Power of Our Words: Teacher Language That Helps Children Learn* by Paula Denton, EdD, 2007, www.responsiveclassroom.org.

Model respectful and assertive responses to meanness and bullying

Research on bullying shows that classmates can—and sometimes do— step in and effectively stop bullying and gateway behaviors. But why don't they step in more often? There are many reasons, but one of them is that students aren't sure whether or not the behavior they're witnessing is OK. When they see adults letting it go, they learn that they should also do so. On the other hand, when you practice respectful and assertive ways to stop cruel behaviors, you set a standard of kindness and let students know that they shouldn't let mean behaviors go either.

Furthermore, you're showing children how to take a respectful and assertive stance against meanness and bullying. The Olweus Bullying Prevention Program states, "When children see adults taking positive action against bullying behavior, it empowers them to do the same" (Olweus et al., 2007, p. 33). By their actions, teachers can give a clear message that any kind of mean behavior is unacceptable.

At the same time, it's important to model respectful behavior toward all students, including the child who is being unkind. If you stop mean behaviors with disrespect, a harsh tone, or sarcastic words, you can escalate the climate of disrespect. When you calmly and kindly redirect students who are exhibiting mean behavior, you model behaviors that promote a climate of respect.

Here are two ideas for how to do this. I'll explain each in detail in the following pages:

- "Go public" with redirections and interventions for unacceptable behaviors.

- Use logical consequences to show students that you expect them to take responsibility for their actions and change their behavior.

"Go public" with redirections and interventions for unacceptable behaviors

When Julia announced loudly "I'm not sitting near Louis; he smells," Mrs. Cohen responded firmly, in front of the whole group, "Everyone in this class is part of our community. Our rules say we will include everyone. Julia, make a space for Louis in a friendly way." Mrs. Cohen's firm, respectful, and direct tone and words showed the class that exclusion was unacceptable. She did not belittle or threaten Julia. Nor did she take Julia aside to give the redirection. Research shows that such adult behaviors promote bullying (Olweus, 1993).

When Mark called Harry "Hair Ball" during a math lesson, Mrs. Larsson said firmly to Mark, "Mark, rewind and use Harry's name when you speak to him." The next day, Mrs. Larsson held a class meeting about using people's names as they want them to be used. She didn't humiliate Mark by stating that the meeting was about his behavior. She didn't humiliate Harry by announcing to those who might not have heard that someone had called Harry "Hair Ball." She simply said, "We have an important issue that we need to discuss." Children who had heard Harry referred to as "Hair Ball" knew perfectly well why they were having the meeting. Those who had missed the name-calling just knew that Mrs. Larsson cared a lot about people's names being used in a respectful manner.

Use logical consequences to teach students to take responsibility for their actions

Bullying is a serious matter, and it is of vital importance that teachers protect children by stopping mean behaviors in their tracks. Logical consequences are one tool that will both stop mean behaviors and help students learn a different way to behave.

Keep in mind, however, that logical consequences are not a form of punishment. Unlike punishment, which can give a message of "You're bad," logical consequences give the child the message that she has the potential to stop mean behaviors and make positive changes. The goal with logical consequences is to teach children a better way to behave, not to shame them or make them feel bad.

The research on bullying shows that taking a punitive approach, all too common in today's "zero tolerance" climate, is ineffective or, in some cases, actually promotes bullying (Rigby & Bauman, 2010). When children are treated punitively, they have a model of disrespect. In addition, when children are punished, their resentment can escalate.

To use logical consequences effectively, in a nonpunitive way, pay attention to the following guidelines:

- Be sure consequences are related to the misbehavior

- Deliver consequences respectfully

- Be sure consequences are proportionate to the misbehavior

Be sure consequences are related to the misbehavior. Consequences that are related to the misbehavior help children make the connection between the action and the consequence. Gateway behaviors to bullying are, by their nature, social. They encompass spreading unkind rumors, calling children cruel names, and excluding children from play. Even when the behaviors are physical ones such as hitting, hair pulling, and pinching, they are, at root, a social assault. For that reason, many consequences will involve removing the child who has engaged in these behaviors from the social situation.

If a child is mean to others on the bus, she'll need to sit next to the bus driver for a few days. If a student throws a ball directly at another student during PE, he'll lose the privilege of throwing the ball for the day. When Martine and Lucy told the other girls not to play with Suzanne at recess, their teacher, Mr. Stegman, explained that they would both lose the privilege of playing with others at recess the next day. In addition, he separated Martine and Lucy so they lost the opportunity to socialize with each other. In all these cases, the teacher will check in with each child about the misbehavior and discuss and practice more pro-social ways to behave before the children regain the social privilege that they temporarily lost.

Exclusionary behaviors are about how children choose whom to be with and whom to leave out. For that reason, it's often a logical consequence for children to lose the privilege of choosing, whether partners, teams, or work groups. When, despite class meetings about fair teams, Malik, Andrew, and Finn, the class athletes, arranged things so that they were always on the same kickball team at recess, playing against the less athletically accomplished students, Mrs. Young told them that they'd lose the privilege of picking teams and she would assign them to teams for a few days.

Besides being social, gateway behaviors to bullying are also, by their nature, unkind. For that reason, logical consequences might involve practicing acts of kindness. If an older child bothers the kindergartners on the school bus, the consequence might be to go to the kindergarten room and, under the kindergarten teacher's close supervision, kindly help the children put on their snowsuits before dismissal.

Deliver consequences respectfully. Consequences that are calmly and respectfully delivered model a respectful way of relating to others. Some children who bully have been subject to disrespectful treatment themselves. That's the model they're familiar with. It's important to show them a better way. Furthermore, if you humiliate children, they will be resentful and possibly focus on revenge rather than how they might do better next time. Mr. Stegman was calm and matter-of-fact as he explained, "You won't be able to play together at recess tomorrow, Martine and Lucy."

Be sure consequences are proportionate to the misbehavior. When you use consequences to underscore the importance of friendly and respectful behavior, it's important that those consequences be proportionate to the misbehavior. Mr. Stegman didn't tell Martine and Lucy to take a break, as he sometimes did when students didn't follow the rules in a tag game. Telling others not to play with Suzanne was far more destructive than breaking the rules of a game. Nor did he tell them that they'd miss recess for the rest of the year, which would have been disproportionately punitive.

For more information about logical consequences, see *Rules in School: Teaching Discipline in the Responsive Classroom*, 2nd edition, by Kathryn Brady, Mary Beth Forton, and Deborah Porter, 2011, www.responsiveclassroom.org.

When children deny culpability

Perhaps you've heard the denials: "But I didn't do anything—you just like to pick on me." Studies have shown that many children who bully do not feel remorseful about their behaviors. Some believe that they have every right to insult, exclude, or otherwise harass others (Davis, 2007a; Olweus, 1993). When Mrs. Sharpe spoke with Wayne about his badgering of Jackson, Wayne's response was, "But Jackson's such a dork. He deserves it."

It's important not to engage in the "I didn't do anything" discussion. Simply stating class and school rules, employing a consequence, and then moving on gives the message: We do not treat people that way in this community.

Perhaps you've heard the complaints: "But it's not fair; other kids do that and you don't say anything." That's why it's vitally important to make sure that consequences are delivered even-handedly. When Mikal and Jerome, usually kind to all, tried out excluding others on the playground, giggling wildly, "Don't play with Sam, he's a retard," Mr. Stegman calmly explained to them that they wouldn't be able to play with others at recess tomorrow, and he'd be watching them during the next week to make sure that they were kind to everyone. When Martine and Lucy showed similar exclusionary behavior, the consequence was the same as Mikal's and Jerome's. The children could see that the rules and consequences apply to everyone.

Strategy in Action:
In the Midst of Change, a Second Grade Teacher Responds to Misbehavior

Over the summer, the school district where Mr. Harrison teaches second grade went through a redistricting. This fall many children are attending new schools. Along with changing bus routes and new faculty configurations, everyone is dealing with different student groupings. Research shows that bullying peaks in new groupings where children are establishing a new social hierarchy (Pellegrini et al., 2010). Who will be friends with whom? Who will be "in" and who will be "out"? Who will be "popular"?

It's November. Although Mr. Harrison spent time at the beginning of the year building community, he's noticing an increase in mean behaviors. For example, three boys have begun to roll their eyes whenever another boy speaks in class. Mr. Harrison knows that he needs to put a stop to this behavior. He has ▶

a serious talk with the boys, making sure to stay calm and nonjudgmental. He refers to classroom rules and points out that the class has agreed to take care of each other. He listens carefully to each student's point of view. Then he says, "I expect you to follow our classroom rule to take care of each other. That means that you will be respectful listeners when anyone in the class is talking. I will be watching to make sure you do that. I know you can."

Mr. Harrison has also noticed that four of the girls in his class have begun to call themselves "The Cliquettes." He heard one girl say to another, "I'll be your friend if you don't play with Leslie."

He knows he needs to talk with the girls and decides to meet individually with each one because he doesn't want to reinforce their exclusive bonding. When he talks with them they each nod their heads and agree to do better, but the next day he sees Shavonne wandering the room to "sharpen her pencil" while whispering to various girls. He finds a note crumpled up on the floor that says, "You're ugly. You can't be one of the cute girls."

Mr. Harrison can see that he needs to do more to stop the "Cliquettes'" mean behavior immediately. He begins by separating the four students, realigning table groupings so that they sit far away from each other. He also informs other teachers who work with his class that the girls will be separated for a period of time. He tells each girl why he will be separating her and that he will be watching her and noticing incidences of kind and inclusive behavior. They'll meet in a few days to evaluate how things are going.

Mr. Harrison continues to intervene in small acts

After these incidents, Mr. Harrison realizes he needs to use firm and immediate consequences for the smallest acts of disrespect. The first time a student rolls his eyes or passes an unkind note, Mr. Harrison will stop the behavior with clear language, referring to classroom expectations followed by a consequence. "Max, stop that. In this class we use respectful body language," will be Mr. Harrison's first response. If Max continues the eye rolling, Mr. Harrison will calmly and respectfully separate Max from the group.

Mr. Harrison revisits community-building activities

Mr. Harrison also decides to bolster the class's work on community building. He'll revisit some of the activities that he used with his students in the beginning of the year. The children will play singing and clapping games that get them moving around, relating to nearly everyone in the class. He'll infuse academics with a community-building focus as well.

Mr. Harrison decides that this would be a good time for a whole-class poetry unit. Children will search poetry books for favorite poems to share with classmates. They'll memorize some poems as a class and recite them chorally. They'll write poems and share them with classmates, all under close supervision to keep things friendly and kind.

Mr. Harrison also decides that this would be a good time for the whole-class math unit on graphing. Children will interview each other about favorite hobbies, with careful emphasis on asking kind and respectful questions. They'll create graphs and share them with the class.

Throughout these community-building activities, Mr. Harrison uses language to nurture a climate of caring among his students. "What have we learned about classmates today?" he asks after children have concluded interviews about their hobbies. He reinforces caring behaviors with such language as "I've noticed people listening to each other so carefully."

Soon, Mr. Harrison's comprehensive approach proves to be effective. By reestablishing expectations of positive behavior and responding quickly and directly to misbehavior, he is able to create a kind, caring classroom community. ∎

Communicating With Parents About Misbehavior

In the following chapters, I talk about ways to keep the channels of communication open and build trust with parents. This work includes talking with parents about your efforts to create a safe and caring classroom, your approach to creating classroom rules, and how you respond to misbehavior. In addition, be sure to invite parents to ask questions and share information that could help you effectively teach their child. This is important work that needs to begin in the first days of school and continue throughout the year.

One area of communication that needs particular tending is communication about bullying and gateway behaviors. Teachers need to hear from parents when parents see or hear about mean behaviors between their child and others in the class or the school. And teachers need to keep parents informed about behaviors they see in school and about how they're responding. If you regularly give parents information and give them opportunities to share information, they'll be more likely to trust that you care and want the best for their child—and if a bullying situation that involves their child ever comes up, the communication will go more smoothly.

Over more than thirty years of teaching, I've figured out some guidelines for how to keep communication about these difficult situations open and positive.

Hearing parents' concerns

Unkind behavior, especially bullying behavior, often goes on under teachers' radar. The spitball is tossed or the hair is pulled when our backs are turned. The student is "un-invited" to the birthday party in the hall on the way to the school bus. We have no firsthand information about what children are doing to each other in the online environment. Research shows, and my experience supports, that parents are more likely to know about bullying and other mean behavior than we are (Olweus & Limber, 2010). Parents also know about bullying situations that happen at home or in the community and that can spill over into the classroom.

If parents don't let you know about these behaviors, the meanness can spiral out of control. However, if you've established clear channels of communication, parents can give you valuable insight into students' lives both inside and outside of school and be your ally in bullying prevention work.

Listen, assess, and communicate your observations to parents

When parents contact you with information about mean behaviors they've observed at home and in the community, listen and assure them that you will carefully observe the students involved to see if the mean behaviors are occurring in the classroom. You then need to follow through with a phone call to the parents to let them know what you've observed and how you are going to respond. For more about communicating with parents about outside-the-classroom mean behaviors, see Chapter Five.

Parents will also hear about and report to you incidents that happen at school, and it's important to take these reports seriously, even if you think the child is embellishing a small incident. For example, Janine might complain to her parents that "Lori rolled her eyes at me in school today." Janine's parents are concerned and call you. You need to receive their report seriously and then observe carefully.

If, when you watch, you see no such put-down behavior and observe that Janine and Lori actually work well together, you can respectfully let Janine's parents know. Your observations might reassure Janine's parents that the eye-rolling was a small, one-time incident.

You also need to let Janine's parents know that you will continue to watch Janine's and Lori's interactions and that you want to know right away if they hear anything more about disrespectful behavior. When you communicate your appreciation of their reports and emphasize your commitment to respectful behavior in the classroom, you increase the likelihood that parents will stay in contact and let you know about potentially harmful events.

Set the stage so parents feel it's OK to report concerns

Note that in this example about Janine and Lori, the positive outcome was possible because Janine's parents felt comfortable bringing a complaint to the teacher in the first place. It's important to set the stage so that parents feel it's safe and productive to approach you with a potential problem. In Chapters Two, Three, and Four you'll learn about establishing open, trusting communication with parents in the first days and weeks of school.

Notifying parents about student misbehavior

Just as teachers need to hear from parents about outside-the-classroom behavior, parents need to hear about the inevitable mean behaviors that occur in the classroom. How you let them know, though, makes a big difference in how supportive they are as you and your school work to solve the problem. Here are some things to remember.

Wait until you're calm

If you're angry or annoyed about a student's behavior, wait until you've calmed down before contacting the parents. I'll never forget the moment in my classroom when Jimmy pinched Christa on the bottom. I went right to the telephone and called Jimmy's mother. My frustration and annoyance crackled right through the phone line. Jimmy's mother was understandably protective of Jimmy. Although I eventually repaired my relationship with Jimmy's mother, she never did see the bottom-pinching incident quite the way I did.

Begin with the positive

No matter how negative the event, it's always possible to begin with something positive. Madelyn may be circulating around the classroom loudly whispering "You dork" to her perceived "enemies." It's still possible to start by saying truthfully, "Madelyn's reading skills have improved in the past month," or "Madelyn always has a joke or a cheerful comment for me when she arrives in the morning." More than anything else, parents want to see that you like their child. With that established, they can more easily hear about their child's imperfections.

Avoid labeling

No one wants to hear that their child is a bully. If you use that word, you set parents up to feel defensive and stop listening to the information that you're hoping to communicate. Better to describe the behavior as specifically and concretely as possible. "Yesterday, during Social Studies, Mike told Jamie his map looked 'stupid' and said he didn't want Jamie to be part of his workgroup," is specific and succinct. Leave out such embellishments as "with a mean smile on his face" or "in a bossy way." Be matter-of-fact about the behavior. If you convey that Mike made a mistake that's been made by many other children, you're far more likely to enlist his parents' cooperation than if you convey indignation and outrage.

Provide evidence

If parents are disbelieving, concrete evidence may help. When the third grade girls started directing, "Don't sit next to Katie on the bus," the bus company actually had a videotape of the bus behavior to share with the parents of the children involved. Of course, not everyone has school bus videotapes. You may, however, have the actual note that a child sent or other such evidence.

Inform parents but retain responsibility for solving the problem

Once everyone understands what happened, it's unreasonable to put the burden of solving the problem back on the parents, just as it would be unreasonable for a parent to expect you to get their child in bed on time. It's more realistic to hope for support or, at least, lack of resistance, as you and your school solve the problem.

It's also important to let parents know how you are going to respond. For example, "Faye cannot ride the school bus for a week because she told others not to sit with Katie" or "Mike will need to work alone during Social Studies for a few days."

Maintain confidentiality

When several children are involved in an incident, parents often want to know what consequences you're employing with the other children. It's fine to simply say that you are addressing the problem with every child. Don't violate confidentiality by going into specifics about your interventions. If you have any questions about confidentiality in your situation, check with your school or district.

K e y   I d e a s

"Focus on the small stuff"—notice and stop small acts of exclusion, mean words, and seemingly casual swipes before they become major incidences of bullying that are far more difficult to turn around.

Take time to observe students both in the classroom and in other settings so that you're aware of the behaviors they're engaging in.

Use respectful consequences immediately for small "gateway" misbehaviors.

Listen carefully to parents' concerns.

Notify parents about children's misbehavior.

Chapter Two

Helping Children Get to Know Each Other

• • •

*T*he students in Mrs. Meyer's third grade class are getting ready for the morning. James is sharpening classmates' pencils. He pauses to exchange a quick high five with Lenore as she enters the classroom. Shari is busy checking people's homework. "You remembered, today," Shari congratulates Kendra, who often forgets her homework. Markeith sees that Lewis, who uses a wheelchair, is approaching the classroom door. Markeith checks the furniture to make sure that there's space for Lewis's wheelchair and then goes to meet him at the door. "Hi, Lewis," he says. "Did you watch the game last night?" He knows that Lewis is an avid basketball fan.

Mrs. Meyer's students welcome each other into the classroom each day. Mrs. Meyer takes deliberate steps to ensure that students know each other's names and greet each other kindly and respectfully. She structures opportunities for students to share information about their lives and to have fun together. She knows that teachers who have reduced or prevented bullying are teachers who have focused on creating a positive climate in their classrooms and in their schools, a climate where every student is known, honored, and respected.

From day one, these teachers take steps to build a strong, inclusive classroom community. They pay attention to how children treat each other. They help children get to know each other and learn to work and play together. They set expectations that each student will work and play with every other student. The work that begins on day one continues throughout the year.

The importance of these teachers' efforts is backed up by the research on bullying, which shows that children are less likely to engage in bullying behaviors if they feel connected to their peers, to their teacher, and to the school as a whole. Research also shows that children who are targeted are often the children who are isolated from the group (Pellegrini, 2010; Rodkin & Gest, 2011).

Teachers can begin with the most basic step of helping children learn each other's names and give them opportunities to learn about each other's lives. When we do this, we are also helping them practice empathy, value differences, and understand the importance of being friendly to all, even if they're not going to be best friends with everyone. We then can encourage and support them as they make hard decisions about behavior.

In this chapter, I focus on the following topics:

- Helping children learn each other's names

- Helping children get to know each other through structured greetings, sharing, and group activities

- Integrating "getting to know you" activities into academic structures

- Communicating to children's parents that you care about creating a caring and inclusive classroom and want to work with them in ongoing ways to achieve this goal

Begin With Learning Each Other's Names

It's easy to assume that children will take the initiative in meeting their classmates. However, in my experience, children may know only the names of others who live in their neighborhood, who ride their bus, or whose families are family friends. Those are the children they speak to, sit with, and play with on the playground. Without deliberate "getting to know you" structures, the children who are comfortable with each other get to know each other better and better while other children stay on the margins of the social networks in the classroom, which leaves them vulnerable to the type of mean behavior that can lead to bullying.

Use name tags or cards in the first weeks of school

Making sure that everyone learns everyone else's name is the first step toward creating an inclusive classroom. In many schools, children and adults wear name tags for the first six weeks or so of school. In addition, children label their tables, desks, and lockers or cubbies with personally decorated name cards, and children's names are prominently displayed on attendance charts.

The use of name cards or tags is valuable at all grade levels, not just in primary-grade classrooms. Sometimes we assume that older children won't need name tags because they know each other from previous years. Some do know each other, of course, but some don't. In addition, older children will often gravitate toward children who are familiar, whose names they know, whom they've seen before. The children whose names they don't know will become the marginalized children, the children who might be targeted for bullying.

To make the name tags in early grades, when children are just learning to read, teachers might ask children to bring a photo to school, or take children's photos themselves when children attend meet-the-teacher day. Teachers can then augment each child's name tag with a small copy of her or his photo. Older students might want to decorate their name tags with drawings of their favorite activities, symbols that indicate something about them, or other decorations that make the name tags theirs.

Structure opportunities to practice kind behavior

The introduction of name tags also provides an opportunity to begin guiding children toward kind and helpful behavior. Mrs. Velasquez greets the earliest arriving of her third grade students with directions to find their cubbies, put away their belongings, find their labeled seat, and begin to decorate their name tag. As subsequent children come in, she asks the early arrivers to show the more recent arrivers how to complete these routines.

Down the hall Mr. Rinaldi, a kindergarten teacher, places name cards on tables. As children arrive in the classroom, he greets them warmly at the door and directs them to find their name at a table. Miss Snyder, the music teacher, is there to help, guiding children toward their name card, helping them get started coloring a picture, and directing them to help each other. "Julius, this is Natasha," she says as Julius finds his name card next to Natasha's. "Natasha, would you show Julius where the crayons are?" she asks.

Through these small steps, Mrs. Velasquez and Mr. Rinaldi send the powerful message, "In this classroom, we help each other. In this classroom, everyone is important. In this classroom, kindness rules."

Help Children Get to Know Each Other

Learning names is an important first step. But to prevent bullying, we teachers need to go beyond simply making sure that children know each other's names. We need to help them get to know each other in a climate of safety and support. We need to build an inclusive community where everyone belongs and where everyone has a role, just as Mrs. Meyer did in the opening paragraphs of this chapter. The best strategy that I have found to create this caring climate is the *Responsive Classroom* strategy of Morning Meeting. In Morning Meeting, everyone in the classroom community gathers in a circle each morning to greet each other, share news about their lives, take part in an activity together, and read a posted message from the teacher.

In the following pages, I'll give information on helping children get to know each other better by using strategies based on Morning Meeting structures. If you don't do a *Responsive Classroom* Morning Meeting, you can still adapt these ideas to fit your classroom schedule and structure.

Set up greeting routines

There's great power in beginning every day with each child greeting classmates and being greeted in turn. Setting up a whole-group structure for this kind of beginning is an important way that you can help children get to know each other and feel that they belong. Early in the year, these whole-group greetings can be as simple as a friendly "Good morning," coupled with a classmate's name, making its way around the circle. As children become comfortable with this basic greeting, you can add in a handshake or a high five.

Later in the year, you can add in other challenges such as having children greet each other across the circle, combined perhaps with tossing a ball or other soft object. Whatever structure is used, as each student's name is stated, the student is brought into the circle of the community. When everyone is part of that circle, the potential for any individual to be treated meanly is dramatically reduced.

Build in time for greeting, every day

A daily morning gathering such as Morning Meeting is a highly effective structure for ensuring that students greet each other every day. However, even if you don't use such a daily gathering, you can set aside a few minutes for a quick greeting early in the school day.

Mr. Rinaldi, the kindergarten teacher mentioned above, waits until everyone has arrived. Then he gathers the children in a circle on the rug and leads the class in a simple song that uses each child's name. "Where, oh where is our friend Natasha?" Mr. Rinaldi sings. The tone is set: Natasha is our friend. Children who feel ready join in as he repeats that line three times. Natasha may stand, wave, or simply smile to show where she is. Students then sing "Way down yonder in the paw-paw patch" before Mr. Rinaldi sings "Where oh where is our friend [classmate's name]" to name the next student. On they go until everyone has been named.

State the purposes of greeting

Greeting each other every day is a powerful way to bring everyone into the classroom community. It could backfire, though, if children greet each other in ways that further unkind agendas. To keep greeting safe, teachers need to teach the purposes and skills of greeting each other respectfully and inclusively.

The first step is to tell children why they are greeting each other every day. Be explicit about building a sense of safety. For example, you could say: "We'll greet each other every morning so that everybody feels welcome in our class." When children understand the purpose—that greeting each other contributes to everyone's feeling included in the classroom community—they will be more likely to stay invested in keeping greeting safe and friendly.

Throughout the year, teachers might also need to periodically remind children of the purposes of greeting. "Remember to take care of our rule to be kind and friendly as we greet each other this morning," a teacher might say. Or, "Remember, we greet to make everyone feel welcome. What does it sound like when someone makes you feel welcome? How can you make your greeting partner feel welcome this morning?" Whatever the behaviors that you expect from children, they need frequent reminders to keep that positive energy flowing.

Teach and practice the skills needed for greeting everyone in a respectful, friendly way

Next, children need to learn *how* to be respectful and friendly to those they don't yet know very well. Show children what a respectful, friendly greeting looks like and sounds like. Model how to greet someone with a smile. This is a great time to use the *Responsive Classroom* strategy of Interactive Modeling described in detail in Chapter Four.

To build students' investment in being respectful and friendly, help them tap into their own thoughts and feelings by reflecting with them. "How might it feel when someone greets you with a smile?" or "What can you do to make your greeting partner feel welcome in school?" are questions that you might ask.

In Ms. McCabe's fifth grade class, students gather in a circle each morning for Morning Meeting. Throughout the year, Ms. McCabe introduces a variety of greetings. With each new greeting, she takes time to discuss how to do the new greeting in a respectful, friendly way. "What does a friendly greeting look like?" Ms. McCabe asks. "How do we shake hands in a friendly way?" "What does a gentle high five feel like?" Even fifth graders need to know exactly what is expected if they are to maintain a climate of respect for all. After the class has successfully completed a greeting, they briefly reflect on how they felt as they greeted and were greeted.

Plan and structure greetings that include everyone

If one of the purposes of greeting is to build an inclusive climate, it's important that children greet a wide variety of classmates. When Mr. Sailor says to his students, "Greet three people whom you haven't spoken with yet this morning," he's making sure that his fifth graders greet someone who is not their best friend. When Mrs. Ianello has her first grade students count two people around the circle, greet the third, and take that person's place while that person begins another round of the greeting, she is mixing her students up, ensuring that students greet someone other than the person they chose to sit next to. Such practices foster an atmosphere of inclusion, vital to preventing bullying.

Continue with greeting all year long

To maintain an atmosphere of welcome and friendly inclusion in your classroom, it's important to keep the greeting routine going all year long. You'll likely find that students miss greeting each other if you skip a day.

Certainly, if I had ever forgotten to begin the day with our greeting, the students would have quickly reminded me.

Children often bully children whom they perceive as outsiders. Knowing each other's names and then using people's names in a welcoming, friendly way, every single day, is one part of the systematic effort teachers can make to prevent the formation of a culture of "outsiders" and "insiders" that allows bullying to develop.

Help children get to know each other through structured sharing

Structured sharing is another important way to help children get to know each other. In a *Responsive Classroom* Morning Meeting, children teach the class about themselves by talking briefly on either an assigned or a self-chosen topic. For example, the teacher might name a topic that applies to everyone, such as "What I want to be when I grow up," or "Something that I'm good at," or "Something that's hard for me." Assigned topics can also be academic, such as a favorite story, a favorite place to do homework, or a favorite mathematical operation.

Alternatively, individual children might choose their own topics, such as something they found on the way to school (a bird's egg or feather, a pretty stone), the death of a pet, their favorite ice cream flavor, or other topics of great interest to children at different ages. Several children might share a few sentences at each session or everyone might have a chance to briefly share something about a chosen topic.

The purpose of sharing is to bring everyone, equally, into the classroom community, so whether or not you use a *Responsive Classroom* Morning Meeting, it's important that all students have an equal chance to share over a short period of time, such as a week or two.

Teach children how to share in a way that connects with their classmates

For sharing to be successful, teachers need to take the time to teach children some specific sharing skills that will help them connect with their listeners: speaking loudly and clearly, making eye contact, and keeping sharing brief but informative. When you teach those skills, children will actually want to listen to one another, will learn about one another, and will begin to build empathy for one another. Without attention to these skills, sharing can turn into an exercise where one child gets to talk, but no one listens and learns about the child.

Modeling is an effective way to teach these skills that are so vital to successful sharing. Mr. Rand begins a modeling session in his third grade class by sharing something about himself. "This year we're going to get to know each other by sharing about ourselves. We're going to share public news, things that we want everyone to know. I'm going to tell you a little bit about my favorite after-school activity," he says. "I'll tell you about my favorite activity in a way that is efficient but gives you some information about me. I love to coach soccer for my son's soccer team." Mr. Rand goes on to elaborate with a few sentences about coaching soccer. Then he asks his students what they noticed. Did he share something public? Was he efficient? Did they learn something about him that they didn't know before?

Students chime in with observations about Mr. Rand's sharing. Tomorrow a student in the class will share some public news about herself.

Teach children how to listen respectfully to others' sharing

When teaching children how to listen to each other, it's important to remind them that the purpose of sharing is to get to know each other and that listening carefully helps them do that.

Furthermore, it's important to break down the skills involved in listening and teach them separately, even for older children. You need to model looking at the speaker, being quiet while the speaker talks, keeping attention focused on the speaker, and remembering what the speaker says.

Teachers can hold children accountable for listening by expecting them to report back what they learned. Playful formats make this task pleasurable. "Listen carefully because afterwards we're going to play a game called 'Who Remembers?'" explains Mr. Wu, a fourth grade teacher.

The class shares "What I like to do after school" in an around-the-circle format. Mr. Wu begins by saying, "After school I like to go to the gym." Sammy, sitting next to Mr. Wu, uses Mr. Wu's sentence stem and says, "After school I like to watch TV." Next Frannie says, "After school I like to ride my bike." Once the class has finished, Mr. Wu says, "Who remembers who likes to watch TV?" Many hands go up. Children are eager to share that Sammy likes to watch TV. Playing "Who remembers" doesn't put anyone on the spot, but it does give many children a chance to share what they heard. It elevates and honors listening to each other.

When children share about themselves, they're opening themselves up to the group, which can feel risky. To increase safety, it's important to teach children how to respond with friendly interest and respect.

"Today people are going to begin sharing about what they want to be when they grow up," explains Mrs. Smarz, a second grade teacher. "You're going to get to share what you want to be when you grow up and you're going to learn what classmates want to be when they grow up. This is important information. How can we make sure that everyone is safe and taken care of while we share?"

Children chime in with ideas. "We can listen to them," says Marty. "We can show an interested face," says Pauline.

"Sometimes someone's idea can strike us as sounding funny," elaborates Mrs. Smarz. "What might we do if that happens?"

"We can make sure we don't laugh," says Jenine. "I don't want anyone to laugh at my idea."

"If we don't laugh," asks Mrs. Smarz, "what *will* we do?"

"Hold your laugh inside and just make a friendly smile?" asks Santiago.

"Good idea," says Mrs. Smarz. "OK, let's go. If people forget and do start to laugh, I'll stop the sharing so that we can keep everyone safe."

With this type of preparation, the students know that they have decided together to respect one another's feelings. Those gateway behaviors, such as snickering about someone else's personal information, have been headed off. And everyone knows that if those behaviors emerge, Mrs. Smarz will stop the activity.

Consider limiting the use of "props" such as toys

When children share about material objects, sharing can become a "bring and brag" session that highlights the income differences among students. When a child brings in an elaborate toy to share, children whose families can't afford such toys can feel left out and further marginalized in the culture of the classroom. Children whose families can afford such toys are linked together. The drawing of such class lines in a group can potentiate bullying (Sweeting & West, 2001).

If you think that young students need a prop to support their sharing, you might allow sharing of objects that students made or found or provide other kinds of guidelines for choosing appropriate objects to share. Mrs. Doukali, a kindergarten teacher, has her students share a favorite book. That way, if someone doesn't bring a book from home, she can help that child pick out a book from the school library.

When you keep the focus of sharing on learning about each other rather than displaying possessions, you help children know and understand each other and in the process develop empathy for others who may, on the surface, seem a little different.

Build in time for sharing even if you don't do Morning Meeting

Even if you don't have a daily Morning Meeting, you can give students opportunities to get to know each other through sharing. Sharing could occur after lunch, during snack time, or at the end of the day. It might occur as frequently as every day or as infrequently as once a week. However you do it, it's important to structure these sharing sessions carefully and to teach children the skills they'll need to be interesting sharers and respectful listeners.

The more students know and understand each other, the stronger their connection to school—and to their classroom community—will be and the more likely they are to both avoid bullying behaviors and protect classmates who are targeted.

Use whole-group activities to build connections

Whole-group activities provide another opportunity to bring all students into the circle of community. In a *Responsive Classroom* Morning Meeting, group activities may be serious or lighthearted. They may involve the direct practice of an academic skill or practice of a skill that is less obviously academic. The important thing is that everyone is able to do the activity and that everyone participates equally in a way that is noncompetitive and fun for all. As children laugh together at a silly game or concentrate deeply to read a poem chorally, in unison, with fluency and expression, they are building those all-important feelings of connection to one another.

In Ms. Farnum's fourth grade, the children are sitting in a circle and have each written a little-known fact about themselves on an index card. Ms. Farnum makes a point of saying, "This is a fact that you'd like to share with all of your classmates." The children circulate, find a partner, and each read their fact to their partner. They switch cards, find a new partner, and read a fact about their previous partner to their new partner. "Did you know that Saul takes violin lessons?" Nora reads to Josie. They switch cards again and Josie tells Leo about Saul and his violin lessons.

In Mrs. Singh's first grade class, the children sing together, "There was a dog, lived on a farm, and Bingo was his name, oh." As they sing they spell out B-I-N-G-O, leaving off one letter in each round of the song. Their faces are smiling, their bodies move softly to the music, and as they enjoy singing together, they are incidentally practicing some spelling skills. Singing together builds community.

Ms. Robatille's fifth and sixth graders have come to the circle with their homework, an index card on which they've written a current event that they've read about in the news. Ms. Robatille begins a rhythm, "snap,

snap, clap, snap, snap, clap," snapping her fingers and clapping her hands. The students join in. They snap twice together and then clap. The first student reads his current event. The class begins the pattern again, and after the next clap, the second student around the circle reads her current event. The activity is lively and engaging. Children listen intently, both to learn about each other's current events and to keep up with the pattern. In the rhythm of snaps, claps, and listening, they are one community.

The feeling of closeness engendered by this type of cooperation protects against bullying. Research shows that marginalized children are most likely to be targeted (Card & Hodges, 2008; Pellegrini et al., 2010). Daily cooperative activities, where every child has an equal role, protect against such marginalization. Research also shows that if children are targeted, that targeting often stops quickly when a peer intervenes (Pepler, Craig, & O'Connell, 2010; Salmivalli, Kärnä, & Poskiparta, 2010), and peers are more likely to intervene when they feel close to the child being targeted.

Plan group activities that foster inclusion

Whole-class activities, taught and supervised by the teacher, are a great tool for building the feeling of closeness that helps prevent bullying. It's important to plan group activities carefully if they are to foster closeness. Activities that help children get to know each other build community. For example, as children play the guessing game "Fact or Fiction" where they share two facts that are true about themselves and one fact that is made-up, the class guesses which are true and which is fictional. Children learn a lot about each other while also having fun.

Activities where children all laugh together engender warm feelings of community. Miss Levine's third grade plays "What Are You Doing?" Sean, the first child in the circle, stands in front of Marissa, who is seated next to him. Sean jumps up and down on one foot. Marissa asks, "What are you doing?" When Sean replies, "Brushing my teeth!" everyone laughs at the intentional mismatch. It's then Marissa's turn to pantomime brushing her teeth while announcing that she's doing a different action, for example, swimming. The next child will then pantomime swimming while stating that she's doing some other action. As the action moves around the circle, the children laugh together while break dancing, twirling around, and doing jumping jacks.

Activities where the group as a whole creates something positive build these same feelings of closeness. Doing a choral reading of a poem can provide a sense of group cohesion. As the class breaks up into small groups to devise gestures to go with various lines of a poem and then reads the poem chorally while sharing their gestures, each small group is contributing to the effort of the class as a whole, creating a beautiful and dramatic reading of the poem.

Teach and supervise group activities

To keep group activities inclusive and kind, it's important to carefully teach and supervise the activities. As with greeting, if you introduce the activity by stating its community-building goal and then reflect with children about ways they might meet this goal, you will increase their investment in making the activity kind and safe for everyone.

Mrs. Singh, in the example above, teaches the B-I-N-G-O song carefully. She starts out by explaining to the first graders, "We sing together to have fun together. What can we do as we sing to make it fun for everyone?"

"Everyone needs to sing," says Jamie.

"Sometimes kids make mistakes when they're learning a new song," says Mrs. Singh. "How can we take care of each other if someone makes a mistake?" she asks.

"Don't laugh at them," contributes Suzanne.

"What will we do if we don't laugh?" Mrs. Singh continues.

"You could say, 'That's OK,'" says Petar.

"You could just ignore it and keep singing," says Monique.

This type of preparation heads off any unkind behaviors that might emerge and keeps the activity fun and safe for everyone. Without this type of preparation, the activity could potentially turn unkind and divisive, contributing to an atmosphere where bullying could take root and flourish.

It's also important to think about the various parts of an activity and plan to protect against possible unsafe moments. When Ms. Farnum cautioned her students to write down facts they'd like to share with everyone, she was protecting them from sharing a too-private fact, a fact that could lead to subsequent unkind teasing.

Build in time for whole-group activities every day

I encourage you to build in times in the day when you and the children do these kinds of fun activities together. Group activities can provide a quick, energizing break between more focused academic tasks or serve as a transition between academic blocks. These activities do not need to take a lot of time and in fact can be done in two to three minutes.

Children who have been taught to function as a cohesive whole in the classroom have less need to create a feeling of cohesion by picking on an "outsider." They already have that feeling of cohesion. When they do see a classmate being picked on, isolated, or taunted, they are far more likely to step in and take care of that person being targeted because he is part of their group. Having even one friend is protective against bullying. Being part of a cohesive group, feeling connected to school and the people in it, is even more protective against bullying (Orpinas & Horne, 2010). We adults have the power to create that feeling in our classrooms.

Interactive Modeling

The *Responsive Classroom* strategy of Interactive Modeling lends itself to teaching children new greetings and activities, how to share respectfully, and how to be respectful listeners during other people's sharing. It's also a good strategy for teaching other skills discussed in this book. You'll find a detailed description of Interactive Modeling in Chapter Four.

Ideas for Greetings, Sharings, and Group Activities Mentioned in This Chapter

Greetings:

→ "Good Morning [classmate's name]" passed around the circle

→ Across the Circle Greeting (walking across the circle to greet a classmate)

→ Ball Toss Greeting (tossing a ball to the person you're greeting)

→ "Where, Oh Where Is Our Friend [classmate's name]?" sung by the class to each classmate

→ High Five Greeting (making a high five with the person you're greeting)

→ Skip Greeting (for example, everyone skips two neighbors and greets the third person in the circle)

Sharing topics:

→ What I want to be when I grow up

→ Something I'm good at

→ Something that's hard for me

→ Favorite after-school activity

→ A favorite book of mine

Group activities:

→ Trade One Fact

→ B-I-N-G-O Song

→ Snap, Snap, Clap (naming current events to a beat)

→ Fact or Fiction (students name two facts and one fiction about themselves; others guess which are facts and which is fiction)

→ What Am I Doing? (pantomime game)

→ Choral reading of a poem

For more ideas and information about greetings, sharings, and group activities, see *The Morning Meeting Book* by Roxann Kriete, 2002; *99 Activities and Greetings: Great for Morning Meeting . . . and other meetings, too!* by Melissa Correa-Connolly, 2004; *80 Morning Meeting Ideas for Grades K–2* by Susan Lattanzi Roser, 2012; and *80 Morning Meeting Ideas for Grades 3–6* by Carol Davis, 2012. All available at www.responsiveclassroom.org.

Infuse Academics With "Getting to Know You" Activities

Dedicating time to "getting to know you" activities is one step toward building that all-important feeling of connection to classmates and teachers. Building such activities into academic lessons is another step you can take. Simple graphs and charts, Venn diagrams, and questionnaires all lend themselves to "getting to know you."

Use surveys and graphs to share information at any grade level

Teachers can create simple surveys that ask questions such as number of siblings or favorite hobbies. Later, children can graph the information they've learned. This kind of activity is appropriate at any grade level, including kindergarten. Kindergarten teacher Mrs. Hauer creates a chart that asks "Do you have a brother or sister?" followed by "yes" and "no" columns. The children write their names in the correct column. Next week they'll indicate whether they have one, two, or more siblings and the class will make a graph of this data. They're learning about each other and also becoming familiar with the concept of charts and graphs.

Use Venn diagrams to learn about each other and discover areas of shared interest

In Ms. Lim's third grade, students work with randomly selected partners to create Venn diagrams, a skill that's part of the third grade math curriculum. The middle section, where the two circles intersect, is for "Things we have in common." The outer, nonintersecting parts of the circles are for "Things that make us unique."

Stacia and José work together on their Venn diagram. Stacia writes her name and "girl" in the nonintersecting part of her circle and José writes his name and "boy" in his. They take turns writing as they fill in the inner, intersecting part. They write "third grader, like pizza, like math, like recess."

As they talk they discover that Stacia likes to read Junie B. Jones books and José likes to read Danger Guys books, so they each label their outer circle. Later on, they'll each share with the class one thing that they learned about the other. All the Venn diagrams then go up on a bulletin board so that all students can learn about one another.

Strategy in Action:
A Fifth Grade Teacher Weaves Together Academics and "Getting to Know You" Activities

It's the first day of school. As Ms. Fillion greets the children, she offers each student a slip of paper from a jar. Each slip has a question written on it: "Are you left-handed or right-handed?" "How many brothers and sisters do you have?" or "What's your favorite food?" and so forth. She directs each student to a stack of clipboards, each with a class list clipped to it. The students begin to mix and mingle, carrying a clipboard and a pencil. They introduce themselves to their new classmates and interview each other about the question on their paper, writing the answers next to each student's name on the class list. Ms. Fillion watches the students and notices that they are smiling and laughing. She can see that they are enjoying speaking with new classmates and learning about each other. As the children move about the classroom, they are practicing the skills of conversation.

Once the class lists are full, Ms. Fillion gives a signal for attention and brings the students to a circle of chairs. She begins with a greeting. "We'll do a greeting every day," she explains. She models greeting Mercedes with a friendly, "Good morning, Mercedes." Students notice that she smiled and made eye contact.

"What might you do if you don't know someone's name?" asks Ms. Fillion.

"You could look at their name tag," suggests Rosa.

"We're ready to go," says Ms. Fillion and the class begins to greet each other around the circle, Mercedes greeting Leo, Leo greeting Rosa, Rosa greeting Felipe, and so on.

Next Ms. Fillion asks a few students to share what they've learned about their new classmates. "Alejandro has seven brothers," Maria shares with the class.

"We have seven kids who are left-handed," Frankie announces.

"Fifteen kids like pizza best," proclaims Elena.

The students are beginning to learn about each other. At this point they're just touching the surface. They will get to know each other more deeply in the coming weeks, setting the stage for an inclusive community where students will treat each other with care and respect.

The next day, at math time, the students begin to create graphs from the information that they gleaned the previous day. Elena's graph is about fifth graders' favorite foods, Frankie's graph about their class's hand preference, and Maria's about classmates' siblings.

When the graphs are finished, Ms. Fillion reviews the skill of summarizing. Then the fifth graders practice the skill of summarizing as they write well-organized paragraphs to summarize the data on the graphs.

Ms. Fillion is ensuring that the students get to know each other. She's giving a clear message that everyone in the class is important. In doing this, she's taking first steps in setting the expectation that everyone will be treated with kindness and respect. She's engaging in vital community-building practices while she teaches math and writing skills that are part of the fifth grade curriculum. By interweaving community building with academic skills, Ms. Fillion is taking a step toward preventing bullying in her classroom community. ■

Enlist Parents in Bullying Prevention Efforts

The problem of bullying is a tough one, and it's unlikely that we'll be able to solve it without allying with children's parents. In fact, international bullying prevention research shows that forging a strong home-school connection is one of the most important things that we can do to prevent bullying (Farrington & Ttofi, 2009). Bullying will continue to go on under our radar until we enlist parents in the effort to keep us informed about children's sense of safety in our classrooms. The first step in building this alliance is to talk with parents early in the year about your plans for creating a safe, caring classroom and your desire for open communication with them.

Be explicit that you care about inclusion and kindness

During your very first contact with children's parents, make it clear that your goal is to make the classroom a safe place for their children. Let them know about the steps you will take to help children get to know each other and to build community. Be explicit that you care about inclusion and kindness. You may be able to give parents this information directly at Back-to-School Night or you may decide to communicate with them through a letter home or a phone call. Whichever format fits with your school and wider community, the message needs to be clear: I care about making school a safe place for learning.

Let parents know that you want to hear from them

Some parents may think that teachers are unconcerned about meanness and bullying. I have heard friends and other acquaintances say "She doesn't care," when speaking of their child's teacher. When they find out that I'm a teacher, they tell me tales of their child's mistreatment in school and ask, "Do you think I should tell her teacher? What if she takes it out on my child?" Unless teachers explicitly tell parents that we want to know, they may not tell us about mean ways that their child is being treated in school.

A kindergarten teacher talks to parents at Back-to-School Night

The kindergarten parents are seated at Back-to-School Night, listening to Mr. Rinaldi tell about the year in kindergarten. He describes what the first days will be like and the ways in which he will help children feel welcomed and begin getting to know each other. Mr. Rinaldi also talks about teaching children how to get along with each other and teaching them how to meet school behavior expectations. He then says, "If your child is to have a good start in school, it's important that he or she feels safe here in our classroom. Sometimes children will tell parents things that they don't tell their teacher. If your child tells you about anything in school that is causing him to feel sad, to feel hurt, or to feel otherwise unsafe, please tell me about it. Please do not hesitate to contact me. Your child's comfort and safety in school is the most important thing to me." Mr. Rinaldi ended the evening with this powerful message.

A third grade teacher writes a letter and calls parents early in the year

Third grade teacher Mrs. Velasquez doesn't have the type of sit-down-with-parents opportunity that Mr. Rinaldi does. She does, however, write a letter that she sends home the first day of school. She welcomes parents to the classroom community, describes some of the community-building activities the children will do in the first weeks of school, and explains about opportunities for parents to join the class for specific activities. She ends the letter by stating clearly and explicitly, "In this classroom I expect all children to be kind to each other. I'm counting on you to help by telling me if you suspect that anything unkind is going on."

Over the next few weeks Mrs. Velasquez takes her class list and calls a couple of parents each afternoon after school. Sometimes she chats with a parent; sometimes she just leaves a message on the phone. She always says something positive that she's noticed about the child, such as "I've noticed that Amaya enjoys math so much" or "Garrick is so helpful to

Bree," a child in the classroom who has multiple disabilities. She also asks the parent if he or she has any concerns about their child's experience in third grade so far. She's setting up channels of communication that will maximize the likelihood that parents will let her know if mean behavior or bullying is going on.

K e y I d e a s

A safe and kind classroom helps prevent bullying.

Structures you put in place on day one are an important ingredient in creating safe, kind classrooms.

Learn each other's names as the first step.

Use greeting, sharing, and whole-group activities to help children get to know each other and build community.

Combine "getting-to-know-you" activities with academic activities.

Parents are potential allies in bullying prevention. Take steps early in the year to talk with parents about what you will do to prevent bullying and invite their participation.

Chapter Three

Creating Classroom Rules

• • •

Students in Mrs. Fox's first grade classroom gather in a circle on the meeting rug. It's the first week of school. So far this week, they have talked about what they want to learn in school this year and are now talking about the rules they'll need to help them reach their learning goals.

"Why do we need rules?" Mrs. Fox asks.

"So that we can have fun," pipes up Sylvie.

"How do rules help us have fun, Sylvie?" asks Mrs. Fox, not quite sure where this is going.

"Because if we don't have rules kids might bully each other and then school wouldn't be fun," Sylvie replies.

Sylvie is right, of course. Rules provide a foundation on which the classroom community can be built and give guidance to children about behavior expectations. Without common understandings about how to behave and how to treat each other, the classroom community will be adrift and full of the potential for mean behavior.

For these reasons, rules are an essential component of bullying prevention efforts. Most evidence-based bullying prevention programs include establishment of rules that let students know that mean behavior is unacceptable. Furthermore, these programs employ daily references to the established rules. Whether children read these rules chorally at the start of the day, hear their teachers mention the rules in the course of learning routines or lessons, or reflect on them at the end of the day, the rules are always there, front and center (Swearer, Espelage, Vaillancourt, & Hymel, 2010).

In my experience, going one step further to co-create rules with students adds the power of student investment to the rules. Children who have worked together to create their rules believe in the rules, want to follow them, and will help each other follow them. In this chapter, I share information about how to co-create rules with students so that they see the rules as an important tool for keeping the classroom safe and kind.

Alternatively, you may decide to create classroom rules yourself and present them to the children early in the year. Or you may decide to use previously established schoolwide rules in your classroom. If you follow one of these procedures, you can build student investment in the rules by reflecting with students about how the rules will help keep everyone safe, how they will help everyone be kind, and how they will help everyone learn. No matter how you approach the rule creation process, it's important to establish classroom rules early in the year, build student investment in the rules, and keep the rules alive, day to day.

In addition to providing guidance to the classroom community about what is and is not acceptable behavior, rules that children believe in help teachers avoid power struggles with certain children. Children who bully often resist adult limit setting about these and other mean behaviors. When teachers refer to rules, supported by everyone in the classroom, children are reminded that it's the rules setting the limits and thus they're less likely to slip into a power struggle with the adult who's enforcing the rules. "Our rules say to be kind; that wasn't kind" seats the locus of limit setting with the rules rather than an adult whim. It also is a reminder that rules apply to everyone—that in this classroom being kind is the socially acceptable choice.

In the following pages, you'll find ideas for increasing the effectiveness of rules. Specifically, you'll learn about:

- Bringing children into the rule creation process

- Keeping rules general, few in number, and stated in positive terms

- Helping children apply the rules to daily life

- Talking with children about how and when to report rule-breaking or mean behavior

Bring Children Into the Rule Creation Process

Over many years of teaching children in a variety of grades and in a variety of settings, I have found that co-creating rules with students in the first days and weeks of school brings the power of a shared vision into our classroom. I used many methods for teaming with students to create classroom rules. I finally settled on the method that many *Responsive Classroom* teachers use as the most straightforward way to build student investment in the rules.

I began by helping each student articulate a learning goal for the year. For example, when I elicited goals from third graders, Alycia said that she wanted to become a better reader and read lots of books. Matt said he wanted to learn new math facts. Sometimes goals were social goals. Shane, who hadn't had many friends the year before, said that he wanted to make a new friend. We decorated the walls with their pictures of themselves attaining their goals. The room was full of hopes for our year together.

With goals named, I then asked, "If we are all going to achieve our goals, what rules do we need?" As students brainstormed a list of rules, they had a lot to say. Past hurts were remembered as Pauline said, "No hitting," and as Samuel said, "Call people by their own names."

I helped students reframe the "no" or "don't" rules into positives by asking questions such as "If we're not going to hit people, what will we be doing with our bodies?" Pauline suggested, "Bodies to ourselves." Investment was building as everyone got their ideas out and listed on the large piece of chart paper in the front of the room.

We then began a process of sorting that long list, grouping the ideas by categories, and naming each category as a rule. We spent fifteen minutes or so each day for a week, distilling our rules down and naming them. The time that we spent increased student investment as they proudly said, "We're working really hard on this." (See table below for an example of this categorizing process.)

Brainstormed Ideas, Sorted Into Categories	Rules
Responsibility for self Pay attention Do your work Listen to each other and to the teacher	Take care of our own learning
Responsibility toward others Keep our bodies to ourselves Include everyone Use kind words Call people by their own names Listen to others' ideas Cooperate with teammates	Be kind to all
Responsibility for the environment Take care of materials Clean up after ourselves Take care of other people's things	Keep our classroom and school beautiful

Finally we had three to five sentences, each naming a class rule. If the students did not mention kindness and inclusion, I made sure to bring it up. For example, I might say, "Do we have a rule that will protect people from mean words?" or "Do we have a rule that will help everyone have someone to play with?" Children easily came up with a rule that would help them feel safe and included.

We posted the rules prominently in the classroom and everyone signed their name at the bottom, testifying that they endorsed our rules.

You may not feel ready to engage in this process. Or you may feel that your students aren't ready to think about rules in this way. This isn't a problem—there are many ways to modify the process while still retaining student engagement and investment. For example, in some classes the students might name goals, but then the teacher might create the rules based on those goals.

In other classes, the teacher creates the rules and then the children discuss such topics as "How will these rules keep us safe?" and "How will they help us learn?" As students reflect, they think about their wishes for a safe learning environment in school.

My colleague Donna Skolnick had her second grade students get into small groups and prepare little plays about how each rule would create a classroom that would be "the way we want our school to be."

As long as you involve your students in some part of the process of creating the rules, you are on your way to having rules that will become the touchstone for life in the classroom community and a foundation for bullying prevention.

For more information about this approach to rule creation, see *Rules in School: Teaching Discipline in the Responsive Classroom*, 2nd edition, by Kathryn Brady, Mary Beth Forton, and Deborah Porter, 2011, www.responsiveclassroom.org.

Keep Rules General, Few in Number, and Stated in Positive Terms

In the process described above, I talk about creating a brief list of general and positively stated rules. It might seem that this won't be strong enough—in order to tackle something as serious as bullying, it's tempting to create a long list of "don't do it" rules. However, when teachers post a long list of explicit and detailed rules addressing all possible misbehaviors, it's all too easy for a child who bullies to say "But there's no rule against pinching someone's nose," for example. In addition, a list of rules stated in the negative can feel constraining and restrictive to children, something to find the wiggle room around rather than something to draw inspiration from.

Creating three to five general rules stated in the positive is more effective. Rules such as "We will be kind to everyone," "We will take care of our classroom environment," and "We will be responsible learners" help children know what to do rather than what not to do. The positive framing of these rules allows children to build a vision of a caring community. The rules communicate that together we will create a classroom that is safe, inclusive, kind, and joyful. The rules will then more likely be something that everyone wants to respect to help maintain that feeling of safety and inclusion.

Help Children Apply the Rules to Daily Life

Providing the rules is a first step. For ongoing effectiveness, however, it's important to keep the rules alive, front and center, in children's daily school life. One way to do this is through ongoing reminders and conversations with the children about how the rules apply to specific situations.

For example, a rule such as "Be kind to everyone" provides an anchor for the class, but to prevent the inevitable mean behaviors that can lead to bullying, it's important to be explicit about application. Before a group activity, a teacher might ask, "If our rule says 'Be kind to everyone,' how will we make sure everyone is included during our group activity?" When a teacher has noticed exclusionary behavior, she might say, "Sometimes people leave others out on purpose. That is not OK in this class. We have a rule that says 'Be kind to everyone.'"

These conversations can be brief and can happen at any grade level. In Mr. Rinaldi's kindergarten class, there are three rules: "We will be kind," "We will do our work," and "We will take care of our classroom." These three simple rules cover most of the challenges of kindergarten. He begins by asking children to think about what being kind might look like and sound like. "Pretend you are sitting at the table and drawing. You are using the blue crayon. The person sitting next to you asks to use the blue crayon to color in the sky in his drawing. What could you do that would be kind?" asks Mr. Rinaldi. Children offer ideas for how they might handle such a challenge.

The children go off to draw pictures of themselves doing kind things. On subsequent days they talk and make drawings about doing their work and taking care of the classroom.

After introducing the rules, Mr. Rinaldi is careful to refer to the rules frequently. As the children line up to go out to recess he says, "Who can remind us about Paul's picture of being kind on the playground?" Lori raises her hand and says, "He showed kids playing together. Everyone gets to play."

Conversations about rules might also focus on helping children understand exactly what some of the more general words mean. The rules in Mr. Shane's second grade classroom are "Be respectful," "Be responsible," and "Be safe." Mr. Shane knows that his students need lots of practice if they are to understand what "respectful" and "responsible" mean as well as how "be safe" applies to the school setting. He knows that adults often use "respectful" when speaking to children as if it means "Follow adult directions," and he wants to clarify the deeper meaning of that word.

Remembering the dictionary definition of respect ("To have regard or esteem for"), Mr. Shane starts out by saying, "Another way of describing 'be respectful' might be 'treat everyone so that they know they're important to you.'" Mr. Shane then leads the class in a discussion of what second graders might do to show their classmates that they're important. Mr. Shane records student ideas on a chart.

Laticia says, "We can help each other find things."

Tommy says, "We can share pencils."

Then, to expand the class's thinking beyond material objects and toward less tangible things such as how they speak to one another, Mr. Shane says, "How could we use kind words to help us show someone that they're important to us?"

Mikey quickly replies, "We could ask, 'Do you want to play?'" and Sylvie suggests, "Do you want to eat lunch with us?"

Mr. Shane agrees, saying, "Those certainly sound like kind words."

Later on, as the students get ready to go out to recess, Mr. Shane says to the class, "Remember Mikey's idea about how to be respectful—be sure to ask anyone who's alone if they want to play." When the children come in from recess, he tells them, "Put your thumb up if you remembered to ask someone to play." Mr. Shane is bringing the rules to life for the students.

In both Mr. Rinaldi's class and Mr. Shane's class, the conversations will continue throughout the year in one-on-one conversations as well as in whole-group discussions.

Explicitly make the connection between rules and bullying or mean behavior

It's important to directly and explicitly connect the classroom rules to unacceptable behaviors such as bullying and gateways to bullying. Otherwise, students really may not know that these behaviors are not acceptable. Because they see, or have seen, others doing these things, they think the behaviors must be all right (Swearer, Espelage, Vaillancourt, & Hymel, 2010).

Furthermore, there is evidence that teachers miss many mean behaviors that occur under our radar (Craig & Pepler, 1998; Olweus & Limber, 2010). Children may imagine that when we don't stop these behaviors, we think the behaviors are acceptable. Teachers need to be absolutely clear that mean behaviors are never acceptable.

Let's say you and the children have created a classroom rule about kindness and inclusion. The children have agreed to follow this rule and are invested in doing so. You've discussed possible applications of this rule by raising such questions as "What would being kind look like on the playground?" or "What would you do to follow our rule to be kind when you see someone who has no one to play with?" or "How can you be kind to a new reading partner whom you don't know well yet?"

The next step is to raise the issue of mean behavior explicitly and directly. You might say, "Sometimes kids leave someone out or call someone mean names because they want to show that they're more important than that person. This is not kind. When someone does that, they are not following our rule."

Especially when working with older children, it's helpful to name the behavior as "bullying" and to define what bullying is. You might say, "Bullying is when someone is mean to someone else. Bullying might be using mean words or leaving someone out on purpose or hitting, kicking, poking, and pinching someone. Bullying might be to someone's face or it might be behind their back."

Notice that I'm suggesting describing "bullying" and mean behavior explicitly as a breach of the class-created, positive vision of "We will be kind." Student investment in "We will be kind" then leads to student investment in "We will not bully."

It might be helpful at this point to write on a sentence strip "We will not bully," and attach it to the class rule "We will be kind" as a visual reminder of this application of the rule and to make it clear to children that bullying behavior is not acceptable.

Use children's books to begin a discussion of rules

Many high-quality picture books for children of all ages describe bullying behaviors in an accurate and accessible way. Another way to open up a discussion about bullying and how class rules can protect students from bullying is to read such a picture book aloud, discussing the book with students as you read. The slight remove of a picture book leads to a discussion that children can engage in without dwelling on the fact that perhaps they have done some of the acts described in the book.

In Katie Couric's accessible book, *The Brand New Kid* (2000), classmates reject Lazlo, the "new kid" in school. Listeners' faces are sad as they hear about the mean things that the children in the story are doing to Lazlo. Ellie has a moment of empathy and asks Lazlo to play. Listeners' faces brighten visibly as Lazlo gets a smile on his face. This shared literature experience has given the class a common understanding that they can live by the classroom rule to be kind and protect each other from bullying.

Appendix A includes an annotated bibliography of picture books that I recommend because they present accurate information about bullying behavior and are appealing to children. In Chapter Six I offer lesson plans that will help you talk with students about bullying. Included are specific discussion questions to use as you share some of these picture books with students.

Some Language to Try

If our rule says "Be kind to everyone," how will we make sure everyone is included during our group activity?

Those certainly sound like kind words.

Remember [Mikey's] idea about how to be respectful—be sure to ask anyone who's alone if they want to play.

How can you be kind to a new reading partner whom you don't know well yet?

Sometimes kids leave someone out or call someone mean names because they want to show that they're more important than that person. This is not kind. When someone does that, they are not following our rule.

Help children connect the rules to cyberbullying

Cyberbullying occurs among even young children. Some elementary school students send each other mean texts and even use other social media to bully classmates. One of the problems is that adults are often somewhat removed from the cyber climate of children's lives. To help children apply the classroom rules to the cyber world, it's important to engage with this climate directly.

One way to do this is to bring social media right into the classroom. Mrs. Mercier, a third grade teacher, creates simple web pages and Twitter accounts for all of the students in the class. She sets up the accounts in a way that allows her to control student access and monitor use.

Having the web pages and Twitter accounts allows the children to practice safe and careful use of social media under her supervision.

First she connects their social media work to rules the class has created:

> **Social Media in the Classroom**
>
> Before creating lessons based on social media use or engaging in conversations about use of social media, become familiar with your school and/or district's policy on use of technology and social media.

Help each other and be kind

Be serious about our experiences

Be responsible with and respect all materials

She decides to create a new list of rules for the class's social media accounts, connected to their class rules, just the way they connected "We will not bully" to their class rules.

She gathers her students in a circle. "Today we're going to start using our Twitter accounts. First we need to think about how to keep ourselves and others safe in the Twitter environment. Let's look at our rules and see how they can help us."

Sara raises her hand. "'Help each other and be kind' will be important," she says.

"How might we help each other and be kind in the Twitter environment?" Mrs. Mercier asks.

"We can make sure we say kind things," says Larry.

"We're going to use our Twitter accounts to give each other feedback about school work," Mrs. Mercier explains. "What if you need to give someone constructive criticism?" she asks.

"Maybe we need to say, 'Be honest but be kind,'" says Maya. "If we need to say something that might sound unkind as a tweet we can say it in person."

Mrs. Mercier writes this idea down on a chart.

Before the children go to work she says, "Remember, be honest but be kind." As the children work on their social media sites, Mrs. Mercier reminds them frequently of their "Twittiquette" rule.

As other issues come up, the list of class-generated rules about using Twitter grows. "Stay on topic when you reply" comes about when students began to ramble. "Re-tweet tweets that you think others should read" comes about after Mrs. Mercier teaches a mini-lesson on re-tweeting as a way to help classmates get information they might need for their work.

The class is invested in cyber safety. They see the connection between the class rules that they worked so hard to create, their Twittiquette that they're creating as a class, and the class's climate of safety and kindness.

Strategy in Action:
Ms. Robatille Tailors the Rule Creation Process for Fifth and Sixth Grade Students

*M*s. Robatille teaches a combination fifth-sixth grade class. Although the sixth graders were with her the previous year, the fifth graders are new to the class. She knows that she needs to begin the year by setting expectations and creating rules with the newly formed combination class. Ms. Robatille also knows that the sixth graders are doing the normal developmental work of separating from adults and establishing independence. For this reason, she needs to handle rule creation carefully so that the sixth graders will take positive leadership as they incorporate the new fifth graders into the group.

Furthermore, the students at this school have engaged in some form of rule creation at the beginning of the year every single year since kindergarten. She wants to make the rule creation process feel fresh and important to them, not simply a ritualized re-creation of something that they did when they were five. To engage all of the students fully, she makes lots of connections between the rules, students' personal goals, and the real life of the classroom.

She begins with a discussion of students' strengths and challenges

Ms. Robatille begins with a discussion about what students are good at. The students are excited. The class hears about sports and academics, family life and friends. Next she says, "There's always room for improvement in whatever we do." The class begins to discuss what might be a challenge for students in fifth and sixth grade. She's careful to protect the eleven-year-old students, who tend to be sensitive, by keeping the topic to "students in general" rather than "what might be challenging for *you*." She finishes this discussion with the concept of a personal goal: "What might you work on improving in school this year?" ▶

Students name goals

Over the course of the next week, students name their goals. Some are academic, such as understanding fractions better, and some are social, such as mentoring a younger student or making a new friend.

Students and teacher create rules connected to the goals

During the second week of school, the class begins to brainstorm lists of potential rules that might help them achieve their goals. Ideas are as concrete as "No interrupting" and "Take care of computers," and as general as "No excluding" and "Help others when in need."

After their hard work at creating a list of possible rules, Ms. Robatille notices that the students need an activity break. The class goes outside to play a cooperative game. Upon returning to the classroom, they discuss what contributed to their game's going so well. Children mention that they supported and encouraged each other, used teamwork, and included everyone. Ms. Robatille adds these comments to the class list of potential rules.

Over the next few days the class combines and tweaks their list until they have created four overarching class rules: "Respect each other and yourself," "Respect the classroom and each other's property," "Use teamwork," and "Be safe."

A game provides an opportunity for applying the rules

At the end of the second week of school, the class goes outside to play a game with another class. Before they leave the classroom, Ms. Robatille asks students to remind everyone of one important classroom rule they might need to take into consideration while playing this game. She makes a point of saying, "What rule will help you treat each other fairly and kindly and stop mean behaviors?" Immediately, many hands go up and students eagerly chime in "Use teamwork." When she asks them what teamwork might look like and sound like, they say, "Encourage and support each other" and "Let everyone have a turn."

After the game Ms. Robatille asks her students what they noticed during the game. Mia says, "I saw James help David up when he fell." Another says, "Kendra did a nice job helping Matthew (a student with a diagnosis of autism) run up and down the field."

Fifth and sixth graders alike feel invested in their rules. They see the connection between the rules up on the wall and their daily classroom life. The rules are theirs, to help them have a good year. Ms. Robatille feels that the time that she has devoted to the process was well worth it. Together they have taken the first steps toward a kind and cooperative multi-age community. ∎

Talk With Students About How and When to Report Rule-Breaking or Mean Behaviors

Rules provide an essential framework for positive behavior. But no matter how carefully the rules are established and practiced, children will still sometimes engage in mean behavior and bullying. Unfortunately, a lot of this behavior goes on behind teachers' backs. We can't stop meanness and bullying behaviors that we don't know about, so we need children to alert us.

But in study after study, children say that their teachers "don't do anything" about bullying (Craig & Pepler, 1998; Olweus & Limber, 2010). Their perception is that we don't care, so they learn not to tell us about it. We inadvertently create this situation by teaching students not to tell. If we could do only one thing to stop bullying in school, the most effective step would be to change the school culture about tattling.

Replace "Don't tattle" with "I can see you know our rule"

When children begin school, often at five years old, they rely on the authority of the adult in charge. They want to know what is allowed and what isn't and expect to get that information from their teacher. As they learn the rules, they begin to incorporate them through what psychologist Lev Vygotsky called "other regulation" (Vygotsky, 1978). That is, they report to the teacher every time they see someone not following the rules that they themselves are trying so hard to follow. This other regulation is a way for them to learn the rules—they're practicing the rules by correcting others. And they're leaning on the teacher's guidance as they practice their knowledge of the rules.

For example, Charlene pushes ahead in line to create a spot for herself in front. "Teacher, teacher," sings out Josie, "Charlene cut in line." That constant other regulation about small things can feel pretty irritating to the adults to whom the children are reporting small infractions. The adults often respond by saying, "Don't tattle."

The problem is that young children don't necessarily know the difference between telling about relatively minor problems like Charlene's cutting in line and reporting instances of mean or intimidating behavior such as Charlene's telling Josie that she has to surrender her dessert every day at lunch. Even adults sometimes have trouble discerning whether any particular behavior is a minor "just let it go" behavior or something that needs a firm response.

My colleague Chip Wood, who first drew my attention to Vygotsky's concept of other regulation, suggests responding to young children's telling about small behaviors by saying, "I can see that you know our rule against cutting in line" or "Thank you for letting me know that you know our rule." These responses honor children's impulse to tell about things that are important to them while not getting overly involved with such relatively minor behaviors as cutting in line.

Teach children how and when to report mean behaviors

It's also important to teach children directly that it is important to talk to a responsible adult when they see or experience behaviors that could escalate into bullying. Children of all ages can learn to report behaviors that are mean, hurt feelings or bodies, or are dangerous or destructive.

Notice that I use the word "report." I'm not suggesting that children need to "report" in an official way as part of an anti-bullying protocol. Instead, I'm using the word as a replacement for "tattling" or "telling." The taboo against tattling is so strong in our culture that it's better not to use the language "tell a responsible adult" because the word "telling" has such negative associations for children (as in "I'm gonna tell on you") and sounds too much like "tattling."

To give children the message that we care about their safety, we need to err on the side of listening when they come to us with grievances that, at least at first, sound like tattles. Abolishing the word "tattle" from our own vocabularies would be a powerful first step. We need to show our students that we do care. Otherwise, mean behavior and bullying will continue to flourish out of our sight, and we will be oblivious.

Be sure there's a response when children report mean behaviors

Another way that adults sometimes give children the message that it's better not to report is by handling their reporting in ways that don't fix the problem or, in some cases, make the problem worse.

Once you teach students to report mean behaviors, they will try out that reporting. It's important that the adults they report to respond assertively and sensitively. All too often, adults at school respond to children's reporting of a problem they're having by saying, "Work it out yourself." This practice can make bullying worse. If you suspect bullying, you need to intervene to stop the behavior and protect the child who is targeted.

If children are asking for help, you need to investigate. What happened? If it's a minor conflict among equals, such as who among a group of friends gets to go first in Four Square, you can carefully help the children practice the skills of conflict resolution. If it's an act of meanness, then it's time to intervene immediately to stop the meanness. However, as I discuss in Chapter One, if you suspect a power difference, don't have the children do a conflict resolution talk.

Responding doesn't mean that you have to share the resolution of the problem with the child who reports unless they're reporting something that happened to them. If they're reporting something they've witnessed, it's fine to say, "I'll take care of this right away." If they're reporting something they've experienced, they'll need more reassurance about how you're going to keep them safe. It's also helpful to say to the child who has experienced meanness or bullying, "If the problem continues, let me know." You may think you've dealt with the situation and meanwhile the behavior continues.

In Chapter Six, you'll find lessons for explicitly teaching children about meanness and bullying. These include lessons about how, when, and what to report. Before you teach these lessons or talk with students about reporting mean behaviors outside of the classroom, it's important that you figure out whom the students need to report to when you are not present. If you have the same recess staff every day, check in with one of the recess supervisors, explain the lessons that you're about to teach, and make sure that the staff members will pass any information about bullying or gateway behaviors to you.

The same advice applies to the cafeteria or other outside-the-classroom settings at school. Schools are full of reporting logjams. The recess supervisor may have heard about the mean behavior, the cafeteria supervisor may have heard about it, but they haven't communicated with each other and with you.

Keep information confidential

Equally important is to keep information that children report to you as confidential as possible. When you speak to a child who is exhibiting mean behavior, it works best to say, "Several different people have told me . . ." or "It's been reported to me . . ." so as not to name the reporter. This is particularly important since children who engage in bullying behaviors might retaliate if they think that someone—either the child who is targeted or a bystander—"told" on them. Confidentiality protects the reporter.

Clarify what happened before you confront

Children who bully often deny that they were involved. First, make sure that you know the facts. Ask the child or children who are reporting the mean behavior a few questions to get a clearer sense of what happened. Have them describe the behavior. When and where did it happen? Was it mean? In what way? What felt unsafe about it? What felt hurtful? Specific information can give you a clear picture of whether the behavior being reported is in fact mean.

Situations can get complicated so listen carefully. The girls in second grade had actively excluded Missy for months. They had called her mean names, spit on her on the bus, and refused to sit near her. When Missy, in her misery and frustration, said "I'm going to get a gun and shoot you," the other girls reported this fact to the principal. Ms. Platz, the school principal, listened carefully to Missy when she was sent to the office for using threatening words. By asking lots of specific questions she uncovered the reality. Being fully informed allowed her to handle the situation fairly and effectively.

Once you know the facts, it's important to be clear, firm, and descriptive when you talk with the child involved in the mean behavior. Be clear in your own mind about the consequences of the behavior—you don't want to get caught up in negotiating. If you allow for wiggle room, the child who bullies may well take it.

When children deny their involvement in mean behavior, I've found it helpful to keep in mind the main goal: to keep the child who's been targeted safe. That means protecting him or her from the child engaging in the mean behavior. And remember that the child who is being mean is the one who needs to be removed from the situation, rather than the child targeted. For example, a teacher might calmly say, "People have reported that you called Paul a 'loser' and told him that you'd punch him if he tried to join the game. As a result, you'll be out of the game for a few days until you can treat Paul as an equal member of our class." Over the next few days, the teacher checks in with the child to make sure he understands how to treat Paul fairly and rejoin the game. This isn't about punishment—it's about keeping Paul safe in school.

Communicating With Parents About Rules

To convince parents that you are sincere in wanting to work with them on the important issue of preventing bullying, you need to let them know about some of the specific steps that you're taking to create an atmosphere of kindness and safety. Sharing information about how you create and support classroom rules is a simple and concrete way of doing this.

First, let parents know that you value classroom rules

It's important to let parents know that you view classroom rules as a strong and positive foundation for building a safe, caring classroom community. In your early communications with parents about how you will keep the classroom safe for all, let them know that the class will have rules to guide children's behavior. Reassure parents that the rules will keep their children safe. If the rules are meant to keep everyone safe, parents are far more likely to let you know if they think that something unsafe is going on.

Let parents know the process you will use for creating rules

Unfortunately, many adults' experience with school rules might have been negative—long lists of things "not to do" often accompanied by a list of what would happen if the rules were broken. Letting parents know about your process for creating positive rules can reassure them that their child's experience will be a positive one.

Communication about how you will create rules can happen during visits or phone calls or via a letter sent home to parents. If you're going to work with the students to create the rules, briefly explain some of the steps that the class will complete and offer a brief explanation of the power of co-creating rules with students.

Telling parents that children have "written and made drawings about their hopes and goals for the year" and that children have "thought about what rules might make their hopes and goals come true" conveys that the rules come from the classroom community rather than from an outside authority figure. Explaining that the children "spent time creating the rules" and are "proud of the work that they've done" lets families know that the children are invested in their hard work to create meaningful rules.

Ask for parents' thoughts about learning goals for their children

You begin to build the lines of communication when you tell parents about what you're doing in the classroom. The lines of communication become even stronger if you ask their opinions, creating two-way communication. Formation of a child's learning goals for the year is a key opportunity for parent input.

Many teachers send letters home early in the year asking parents to suggest one school-based goal for their child. This is a practice that I used for many years in my own teaching. I found that parents' goals told me a lot about my new students. When parents replied that they hoped their child would become more independent about homework completion, I had some information about what might be happening at home around homework. When a parent said that she hoped her child would learn to love math or reading, I understood something about the child's current attitudes toward those subjects.

Sometimes goals were unrealistic, such as when a parent suggested that they'd like their first grader to understand square roots by the end of the year. Even unrealistic goals, however, gave us a point to begin a conversation. Whatever adult family members articulated as a goal, the important thing was that two-way communication had been established. Beginning our conversations around a positive topic such as goals for the year stood us in good stead if it became necessary to discuss more sensitive topics.

Share classroom rules with parents and let them know how you will help children apply the rules

Once the class rules are created, send a copy home with each student. Many teachers ask parents to sign a copy of the rules and send it back to school to indicate that they have read the rules.

It's also important to let parents know that the rules are not empty statements written beautifully on chart paper. Let them know that you will be talking with students in an ongoing way about how the rules apply to specific situations, including bullying. And reiterate that you want to hear about any unsafe behavior that is going on. Knowing the rules can help parents be stronger partners in bullying prevention.

K e y **I d e a s**

Classroom rules are a foundation for bullying prevention efforts.

Find ways to bring students into the rule creation process; co-creating rules with students is a powerful way to do this.

Connect the rules to students' learning goals. This increases students' investment in the rules.

Keep rules general, few in number, and positive—a long list of negatively stated rules can work against bullying prevention efforts.

Talk with students about how the rules apply to specific situations, including situations of meanness and bullying.

Replace "tattling," which has negative connotations, with "reporting" or "talking to an adult."

Encourage students to report mean behaviors they experience or witness.

Work with other school staff to ensure that children's reports of mean behavior will be heard and acted on.

Communicate with parents about your approach to classroom rules.

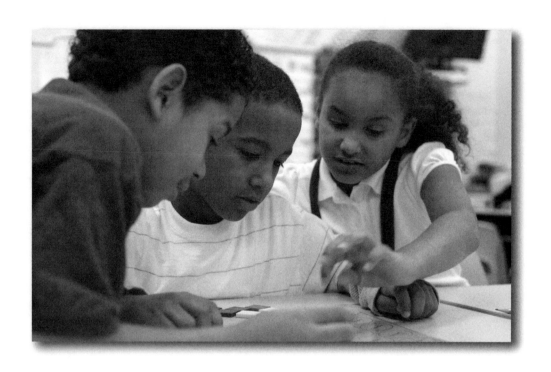

Chapter Four

Teaching Children How to Work Together

• • •

Mandy and Garrick are writing partners for the day. The third graders sit facing each other, ready to review Garrick's most recent draft of his story *Fishing With My Dad.* As Garrick reads the draft aloud, Mandy's face and body posture show that she's listening. She offers relevant comments and suggestions, just as her teacher has taught her to do. Garrick asks questions to be sure he understands her suggestions and makes notes in the margin of his paper. When they've finished talking, he eagerly sets to work creating a final draft of the story which incorporates many of Mandy's suggestions.

Earlier, Garrick was the coach as Mandy read her draft. Like Mandy, he sat quietly, looked attentively at Mandy as she read aloud, and made helpful comments. Working together in this collaborative and respectful way has helped Mandy and Garrick bring their stories into focus and strengthened their writing and thinking skills. It has also given them an opportunity to practice being respectful listeners, a skill they can transfer to other school situations.

There's another benefit to this collaborative work: Children get to know each other. Mandy is not the only student who has seen Garrick's story—Garrick has shared earlier drafts with other classmates as they helped him work through the revision process. As students arrive at school one morning, they rush to tell Garrick about a piece on fishing that will be on TV tonight. "Garrick loves to fish," many children announce. They know because of the work they've done with Garrick on his story.

A key to a strong community is that all students are willing to work with every other student in a respectful way. Whether it's working with one other partner or in a small group, children need to know how to work together cooperatively if a climate of kindness and inclusion is to prevail in the classroom. However, it's not enough to simply group children together and expect them to work collaboratively. In fact, in classrooms where the teacher does not provide sufficient attention to the composition and functioning of the cooperative groups, bullying increases. When socially powerful children are grouped with children who are ostracized, the group provides a rich climate for bullying behaviors (Vaillancourt, Hymel, & McDougall, 2003). In our opening story in this chapter, the teacher considered which children would make effective writing partners, carefully considering whether any particular pairing might feel unsafe to certain children.

In my experience, another key factor is whether or not the children are taught, explicitly, how to work together respectfully. For example, Mandy and Garrick's teacher took steps to teach the students how to give and receive feedback on their writing before sending them into group work. She modeled and had the children practice how to listen carefully, use body language that communicates respectful interest, ask clarifying questions, and give an opinion kindly yet honestly. That's a lot of skills—skills that children don't necessarily bring to school. We need to deliberately teach these skills.

When students work together in small groups without that explicit instruction, things can soon go awry, even if we assign tasks such as group leader and time keeper. Some students become overwhelmed, sit back, and do nothing. Others, in frustration, take over, ordering their classmates to action. Irritation mounts. Soon the arguing begins. Over time, a negative climate takes root in the classroom community. Mean comments and exclusion are regular events and disrespect is the norm.

To prevent this, it's important to break down the skills needed for small-group work and teach each skill explicitly. When children know how to take turns speaking, listen to their partner or group members, respond to what partners or group members say, and keep words, tone, and body language friendly and respectful, children are then able to work together smoothly. Thus the circle of respect grows stronger.

First, Observe the Students

To discover which cooperative work skills students need, carefully observe the children at work as well as in casual interactions. As you watch, analyze which skills students have now as well as which skills they're missing. You can then break the missing skills down into steps that are appropriate for the children's age (see Strategy in Action on pages 98–99 for an example of breaking skills down for first graders). Doing so enables you to make the instruction in partner and group work skills pointed and effective.

Questions to guide your observation

Do all students interact in a friendly, respectful way with one another?

Notice who interacts with whom. Does each student interact with many others during the course of the day? Are some students frequently on their own? Do certain students gravitate to each other over and over? Do students divide up by gender, race, or neighborhood where they live? If you do notice divisions in your classroom, it's time to teach and practice how to be friendly to everyone.

What do you notice about students' body language?

Watch students as they work together. Do they face each other or turn away? Does one group member slowly inch toward another group, as if trying to slide into more appealing company? Does one group member roll on the floor, inattentive while his partner talks? If children aren't using respectful body language, you need to teach and practice what respectful body language looks like.

Do students listen and respond to each other's words?

Listen in on their conversations. It's common for children to conduct parallel conversations, each talking away, sometimes simultaneously, without much regard for what the other is saying. More often than not children will need direct teaching about how to have a conversation before they can successfully work in a small group. Provide direct instruction and modeling about how to listen to what another student says, followed by how to respond directly to the content of a partner's words.

Do students share materials gracefully?

Watch to learn how students manage materials. Do they share writing implements and art materials or snatch them away from each other? Do they hold books and pictures so fellow group members can see, or do they take care only of their own need to see the materials? If you notice students having difficulty, take the time to teach them how to share.

Teach the Skills Needed for Successful Group Work

Observing children and gathering information about group and partner work skills is an ongoing process. As you identify areas that need work, you can use a number of strategies to teach and support needed skills. In the following pages, I'll explain how to use each of these strategies:

- Model desired behavior
- Role-play ways to respond to potentially tricky situations
- Continually name and reinforce ideal behaviors
- Use anchor charts to remind students of newly learned skills
- Use the "fishbowl" strategy to reinforce small-group skills
- Coach individuals and small groups
- Provide structures for taking turns within a small group

Model desired behavior

One of the best strategies I know for teaching the skills children need for successful group work is the *Responsive Classroom* strategy of Interactive Modeling. In Interactive Modeling, the teacher and a few students demonstrate the expected behavior while the rest of the students watch carefully and then name what they observed. In the final step, everyone has an opportunity to practice the behavior while the teacher coaches. Interactive Modeling takes only a few minutes, but because of the students' active engagement in the process, the new learning that occurs is significant.

Here's what the steps in Interactive Modeling might look like when used to prepare fourth grade students to listen respectfully to a partner when working together on a science project.

1. **Tell the class what you're going to model and why.** As a way to increase student investment in doing this behavior, it's important to connect the behavior to the classroom rules. You might introduce the modeling by saying, "Our rules say to 'take care of each other.' When you work on a project with a classmate, you need to take care of each other by listening to each other's ideas. Today you're going to work with a partner to begin to turn one of your 'wonders' about earthworms into an investigation. To make a good start on planning your investigation, you need to listen to your partner's thoughts and ideas." Setting the skill in the context of planning a project such as their first scientific experiment helps increase student investment in the skill.

2. **Prompt all students to watch carefully as you demonstrate the skill.** For example, you might ask a student to talk while you listen carefully to what the student says. (Help the student prepare something to say ahead of time.) To instruct observers you might say, "Notice what I do with my body and my face to let Thea know I'm listening to her." It's important that the teacher plays the key role here to ensure that the modeling shows the desired pro-social behavior.

3. **Ask students what they noticed about your behavior.** Be sure to highlight the desired actions. "What did you notice about my careful listening?" the teacher asks. A student might say, "You looked right at your partner" or "You nodded your head seriously as your partner spoke." Asking students for their observations like this maximizes the likelihood that they will be engaged—and take in the learning.

4. **Ask one or two students to model the same behavior.** You might say, "Yasmine, would you show the class careful listening as Thea talks to you about her ideas?" The teacher in this example has talked to Yasmine ahead of time and helped her practice careful listening so that she'll be ready with some helpful behaviors. But if you know that children have some familiarity with the behaviors being practiced, you can ask for volunteers in the moment.

5. **Ask students what they noticed.** Students might say that Yasmine looked at Thea as she talked, that she nodded sometimes, and that she said "Hmm" quietly sometimes.

6. **Give everyone a chance to practice while you watch and coach.** Assign a simple discussion topic and then form partnerships. You might count off by twos, having the ones listen to the twos first and then the twos listen to the ones. You, meanwhile, can circulate around the room, prompting children to use careful listening. "Remember to look right at your partner, Timmy," or "Listening body language," or "Classroom rules say to take care of your partner" are all words you might use as you remind and redirect.

7. **As students practice, provide feedback, using reinforcing language.** Reinforce signs that students are listening. Feedback can be for the whole class: "I see lots of students looking at each other's faces to show that they are listening." You can also give feedback privately to individual students. For example, you might quietly say to Germaine, "Your eyes are on Rosita. That shows that you're listening to her."

Model only what *to* do

In Interactive Modeling, the emphasis is on what *to* do rather than what *not* to do. You needn't show sarcastic or disrespectful responses. Children are well aware of the negative behaviors—they don't need to see them modeled. They already see cruel and sarcastic responses on television situation comedies. They hear unkind words in popular music. They already have these soundtracks in their minds. Our job is to give them a different, more positive soundtrack.

When we give students a model of what to do, we give them the actions and the words they can use to be kind. When they use those actions and words, they feel the power of positive connections with their classmates. Those positive student-to-student connections are protective against bullying behavior.

For more information about Interactive Modeling, see *Interactive Modeling: A Powerful Technique for Teaching Children* by Margaret Berry Wilson, 2012. Also see *Rules in School: Teaching Discipline in the Responsive Classroom*, 2nd edition, by Kathryn Brady, Mary Beth Forton, and Deborah Porter, 2011, and the *What Every Teacher Needs to Know* K–5 series by Mike Anderson and Margaret Berry Wilson, 2010 and 2011. All books are available at www.responsiveclassroom.org.

Some Language to Try

Our rules say to "take care of each other." When you work on a project with a classmate you need to take care of each other by listening to each other's ideas.

What do you notice about my careful listening?

Yasmine, would you show the class careful listening as Thea talks to you about her ideas?

Remember to look right at your partner, Timmy.

I see lots of students looking at each other's faces to show that they are listening.

Strategy in Action:

Ms. Guerin Teaches First Graders How to Read With a Partner

*F*irst grade teacher Ms. Guerin is getting ready to introduce partner reading. She begins by watching children during arrival time free choice as they look at books on the rug. To successfully read with a partner, the children will need to share the book so that both can see the page. With this in mind, Ms. Guerin pays special attention to the children's use of this skill as she observes. She sees that the children enjoy reading together, but often one child holds the book while her partner, struggling to see the page, peers over her shoulder.

On the basis of her observations, Ms. Guerin decides to teach skills that she has noticed the children are missing. Knowing that she needs to break skills down into bite-sized pieces for children this young, she begins by teaching how to sit so as to share the book harmoniously. She decides to use the strategy of Inter-active Modeling so that children will get to see what this community-oriented behavior looks like and sounds like.

With the children gathered on the rug, Ms. Guerin demonstrates the correct way to sit so that the children see the skill in action. She sits side by side with Charisse and asks the students what they notice about the way she and Charisse are sitting. "Your knees are touching," says Manuel. "Your shoulders are touching," says Marie. "When you partner read," says Ms. Guerin, "you'll sit knee to knee, shoulder to shoulder. You may sit on the floor or in chairs but either way you need to be right next to each other."

Over a series of days, the class goes on to learn other needed skills such as how to hold the book (spine in the middle between you and your partner) and how to decide who turns the page. The task is broken down to its smallest components so that children will know exactly what to do. Ms. Guerin uses Interactive Modeling for each skill—doing the modeling takes just a few minutes each day but goes a long way toward helping the students get ready for respectful partner work.

Once each skill is taught Ms. Guerin immediately gives children an opportunity to practice. She assigns reading partners and the children scatter around the room, practicing reading their books. Ms. Guerin circulates and observes, reinforcing the learning by letting children know when she sees them using the newly taught skills. "I notice you reading with the spine in the middle," she comments to Lucia and Janine. "I see you sitting shoulder to shoulder," she says quietly to Pete and Mikey. ■

Role-play ways to respond to potentially tricky situations

In Interactive Modeling, students learn one way to do something. Through role-playing, students can try out a range of positive responses to potentially tricky situations that could eventually lead to bullying. For example, role-playing could be used to help students think through how to share materials fairly, give each group member equal "air time," or integrate a new classmate into an established work group.

The crucial first step in any role-play is to state the problem in a way that engages the students in positive and community-building thought about solutions. Connecting the challenge to classroom rules that children believe in engages the children in just such a way. You name the ideal when you use statements such as "Our rules say to be kind to everyone. When a new student joins our class, we need to think together about how to be kind to the new student. We need to bring him into our community in a safe and friendly way." These statements get students thinking about how they can help.

Next, teachers set the stage for the role-play (which some teachers refer to as a "little play") by pretending. "Pretend there's a new student in the class and that I'm a student in our class and I'm in a work group for our social studies project. The teacher has told us that the new student will join our work group. Our group has been working together for a couple of weeks. How can I help the new student feel like part of the group?"

The class brainstorms ideas for what the main character—the student— might do. The teacher takes this role in the first round to ensure that things stay positive. Suggestions such as these could go on the list: "You could take a few minutes at the beginning of the day to show him the work that the group has already done" or "You could be his partner during his first work session to help him get familiar with the project."

The teacher then picks a partner to play the role of the new student. Again, the teacher plays the main character in the first round of the role-play to ensure that the demonstration stays positive.

"I think I'll pick taking a few minutes at the beginning of the day," the teacher tells the class. "Lights, camera, action," the class says in unison— a favorite way to signal the beginning of role-plays.

The teacher greets the student playing the role of the new addition to their class. "Would you like me to show you what we've been working on in the social studies project?" the teacher asks.

The class debriefs, responding to focusing questions such as: "What did you notice about our play?" "What did the 'greeter' say and do?" "How did the new student respond?" "How do you think the new student felt?"

Next, pairs of students act out various student-brainstormed ideas, with the class watching and discussing how that idea worked.

Notice that the tone stays positive throughout the role-play. Students aren't acting out the negative, which they know all too well, but rather the positive and pro-social actions that will prevent bullying.

For more information about role-playing, see *Rules in School: Teaching Discipline in the Responsive Classroom*, 2nd edition, by Kathryn Brady, Mary Beth Forton, and Deborah Porter, 2011, and my book *Solving Thorny Behavior Problems: How Teachers and Students Can Work Together*, 2009. Both are available at www.responsiveclassroom.org.

Continually name and reinforce ideal behaviors

In both Interactive Modeling and role-playing, the teacher begins by naming the desired behavior. Naming this ideal, repeatedly, is one way to keep the expectations of kindness and inclusiveness paramount in the classroom culture. I have found that when we connect that ideal to the rules that students believe in, we engage them in working together with energy and enthusiasm.

Mr. Bean, a second grade teacher, assigned new partners for Word Work every Monday. When they began Word Work in September, he used Interactive Modeling to teach students how to be friendly to new Word Work partners. He began the modeling by naming the ideal. "Our rules say that we'll be kind and friendly to all," he said.

Before the children began to work with their new partners each Monday, he reminded them about the ideal by reflecting with them. "Who can tell us what some friendly behaviors toward your new Word Work partner might be?" he asked. As they worked together he circulated around the room. "I see that you're looking at your new partner and smiling at him in a friendly way," he whispered to Patrick.

On Friday, when the children gathered in a circle at the end of the day to briefly look back on their week and wrap up on a positive note, Mr. Bean asked, "What went well this week?" Tommy said, "We were friendly to our Word Work partners." The children were proud of living up to the ideal.

Use anchor charts to remind students of newly learned skills

Once you've taught a skill, children will need reminders. One way to provide those reminders is to work with them to create an anchor chart, a class-created list of expected behaviors or strategies that students can use as an "anchor," referring to it as they need to while they work.

Name the ideal when you ask for children's suggestions

Begin creating the chart by asking children what they know about the skill, being sure to specify the ideal behavior you wish to support. For example, to create an anchor chart about what to do if you didn't understand what your partner or group member said, you might begin by saying, "To have a conversation, we need to understand each other's words. Sometimes people say things that their partners or group mates don't understand. What might be a respectful way to tell your partner that you need her to repeat what she said or clarify her ideas?" Notice that the teacher describes the interaction as a "respectful way." Without this clarity, children might suggest inappropriate ways to talk to their partner.

Whenever possible, use children's own words when you record ideas

To build students' investment in the ideas generated, it's important to use their exact words or, if you need to modify or shorten someone's idea, to ask their permission. However, it's equally important to remember that you, the teacher, are the leader of the class. If someone offers an inappropriate idea, be clear that it is inappropriate. Simply state, "That idea isn't respectful. If someone said that, it could hurt the partner's feelings." Be sure when you do this that your own voice tone and body language are respectful rather than judgmental or sarcastic.

When children offer general ideas, ask for specifics

If children offer rather general ideas, encouraging them to add details can be helpful. Mr. Milner's second grade was creating an anchor chart about how to work with a writing partner. Jordan offered, "We need to be friendly." Mr. Milner wrote down "Be friendly." He then said, "We need some more details here. What does 'friendly' look like?" Children volunteered such specifics as "Smiling face" and "Body turned toward your partner."

Post the chart only as long as it's needed

The anchor chart goes up on the wall. Before lessons or situations that require the skill, you can draw attention to the chart and ask children to read and share ideas from it. But be careful to take anchor charts down when the class has firmly mastered the skill. Otherwise your walls can become so cluttered with anchor charts that children can't focus on current, meaningful information.

Use the "fishbowl" strategy to reinforce group skills

When children are working on social skills to facilitate respectful small-group work, they can benefit from a fishbowl format. In this format, a few students demonstrate a newly learned skill while the rest of the class observes and notes positive examples of the skill. This strategy builds on children's interest in watching each other and contributing their observations. A fishbowl format is especially effective when you've previously taught the skill through Interactive Modeling and children have had a chance to practice it.

Prepare the children who will be in the fishbowl

Advance preparation gives the students a chance to rehearse and gives you an opportunity to make sure that they will demonstrate appropriate behavior. For example, Mrs. McBride has been teaching fifth grade students to work in math groups of four. She asks Phong, Jesse, Lalo, and Catherine if they would be willing to model for the class. "You are going to model one person sharing his or her thinking and the rest of the group asking pertinent questions about how that person solved the problem," she explains. The group huddles for a moment and decides who will be the sharer and what he or she will share about. Then they rehearse. Mrs. McBride watches and notes that the sharing and questions are all on topic and respectful.

Gather everyone into a circle and give instructions to the class

Let students know that a few of their classmates will be coming to the middle of the circle to demonstrate the newly learned strategy. Tell the class specifically what to look for and let them know what they should do when they notice someone using the desired strategy. "You're going to watch a math group," Mrs. McBride says. "One person will share how he or she solved a problem and the others will ask clarifying questions. As they talk, you'll put your thumb up every time you see one of them ask a question that is on topic—in other words, a question that is about how the person who is sharing solved the problem."

Before you begin, prepare the "observers" to treat the "modelers" with respect

You might say, "The group is taking a risk in showing you their process. What do we all need to do to treat them respectfully and considerately?" Students might respond with ideas about listening carefully and stifling impulses to laugh if one of the modelers asks something that seems unrelated to the topic.

After children have observed, discuss the behaviors they noticed

In the example of the fifth grade math group, Mrs. McBride asks such questions as "What were some of the words that you heard students say when they asked on-topic questions about the sharer's work? What body language did you notice that showed that students were listening to each other?"

Finally, of course, it's important to let students know that you'll be expecting them to use this skill in their small-group work. You could say, for example, "I'll be listening for your on-topic questions as I stop by your math groups" or "As I look around the room I'll be looking for respectful and attentive body language, like the body language that we saw in the fishbowl."

Coach individuals and small groups

The discussion thus far has been about whole-class work, appropriate for when you notice that all or most of the students need to learn, review, or practice a particular skill. Sometimes, however, teachers notice that one student or a small group of students are struggling with skills such as using respectful body language, listening to others with interest, or using words that are respectfully related to ideas that others have shared. In these cases there is no reason to re-engage the whole class in learning and practicing skills that they already have down pat.

Instead, meet with the individual or small group. Review or practice the missing skill just as you might review or practice a reading skill when you meet with an individual in a reading conference or a few children in a reading group.

Coach an individual student who is struggling with collaborative work skills

Before the coaching session, take some time to reflect on how you're feeling toward the student. If you're feeling annoyed, your annoyance will come out right along with the teaching, blocking the effectiveness of your instruction. If you're not feeling so positive toward the student (it happens to all of us sometimes) first step back and notice the student's good qualities. Once you feel that you can honestly articulate some positives, set up a time to meet privately with the student.

Following are the steps a teacher might take in coaching an individual student who is having a hard time listening respectfully during peer writing conferences.

1. **State the goal clearly.** Begin with a clear, simple statement of the desired behavior. For example, "We're meeting today to talk about how to have a respectful writing conference with your writing partner."

2. **Be clear about what you've noticed, positive and negative.** Use concrete evidence and examples. Start by describing what is going well and then move to the problem area. "When you share your writing with your writing partner, you read your writing in a way that she can understand. Your voice is loud enough and you say your words clearly. I've also noticed that when it's her turn to read her story you roll on the floor and look away."

3. **State the reasons that the negative behaviors are a problem.** You might go on to say, "Our classroom rules say that we will be friendly and respectful to everyone. To be respectful, it's important that you look at your partner and listen to her read her writing. You need to let her know that you're listening. When you roll on the floor and look away, your behavior is distracting and you seem not to be listening."

4. **Gather input from the student.** You might ask, "What have you noticed about your writing conferences?" This is the point at which the student might say that he is listening, despite the fact that he's rolling on the floor. You can clarify by sharing the information that his partner doesn't know that he's listening unless he's looking at her. At this point the student may also complain about his partner, saying that she's not his friend. You can clarify by referring to the rules and reminding him, "Our rules say that we will be respectful and friendly to everyone. That's your job."

5. **Once the problem is clarified, articulate the desired skill.** Say, for example, "When you listen to your partner, it's important that you keep your body still and look at her. You could look at her face or you could plan ways to share her paper so that you can look at her writing. Either way, you need to show her that you're listening to her with friendly interest as she reads her writing piece."

6. **Show the student what the skillful behavior looks like.** You could listen to the student read a few sentences and then ask, "What did you notice that I did while you read?" Sometimes it helps to

actually write down what the student noticed on an index card so that he can keep the list of skills as a reminder.

7. **The next time the student needs to use the skills, remind him privately of what he needs to do.** Right before writing time, you could quietly and privately say, "Remember, turn your body toward your partner and look at her." Or ask, "How are you going to show friendly interest in your partner's writing today?"

8. **Reinforce positive efforts.** As the students are meeting in partners or small groups, it's important to circulate, observe, and support. Of course, it's particularly important to take a look at the student whom you met with individually. Privately let him know what he's doing well, either with a nonverbal signal like a thumbs-up, or a whispered comment such as "I see you listening to your partner."

> ### Some Language to Try
>
> *We're meeting today to talk about how to have a respectful writing conference with your writing partner.*
>
> *Our classroom rules say that we will be friendly and respectful to everyone. To be respectful, it's important that you look at your partner and listen to her read her writing.*
>
> *When you roll on the floor and look away, your behavior is distracting and you seem not to be listening.*
>
> *How are you going to show friendly interest in your partner's writing today?*

Of course, if you suspect that "She's not my friend" is veering into bullying behavior, your most important goal is to protect the child who is targeted by giving her another partner. In addition, be careful not to have the person demonstrating the mean behavior pair up with his best friend—this could give the message that you're "letting him off the hook."

My book *Sammy and His Behavior Problems* has extensive information about coaching individuals in social skills and group work skills. I also recommend that you take a look at Chapter Two, "Problem-Solving Conferences," in my book *Solving Thorny Behavior Problems*. Both books are available at www.responsiveclassroom.org.

Coach small groups that aren't working together effectively

Although most of the children in the class are working together smoothly in small groups, perhaps there is one group that is struggling. In this group arguments abound and little work is accomplished. The situation is ripe for meanness and bullying.

Watch the group at work. What positive behaviors are they using? What are the negative behaviors? Are there skills that everyone in the group is missing? If all children in the small group are exhibiting similar negative behaviors such as talking all at once, doing other work while group members speak, snatching materials away from their peers, passively staring out into space, or otherwise showing group work skill deficits, think about coaching the group as a whole. Use the same steps and strategies that you used to teach the whole class; for example, name the goal and then model the desired behavior. When a small group of children watch and listen to you teach the skill and then practice the skill under your guidance, it's likely that their skills will improve.

When coaching individuals and small groups, watch for and intervene in mean behaviors

Sometimes in the course of coaching students, you might notice signs of bullying or those small mean behaviors that can be gateways to bullying. For example, if one child in a group orders a particular group member around while others remain silent, or if one child in a pair lobs nasty remarks at her writing partner rather than giving helpful feedback, you'll need to take firm, immediate, and nonpunitive action to stop the behavior.

The first step is to make sure everyone is safe. If a child's unkind behavior is persistent or severe enough to put other children at risk of emotional or physical harm, remove the child who is hurting others from the group or partnership. I can't state this strongly enough: The child who is bullying or engaging in pre-bullying behavior is the child who needs to be removed, *not* the child who is targeted. If you need to end a partnership because of one child's mean behavior, be sure that the child he or she was targeting has another partner to work with. Because there is a strong connection between social isolation and being targeted for bullying, the student at risk of being targeted needs stronger social connections, rather than isolation. The child who is hurting others can take a temporary break from peers.

Talk with the child who is engaging in mean behavior. Begin by clearly and concretely stating your observations. For example, you might say, "I heard you tell Micha to 'be quiet' several times today when your group was working." Avoid such general statements as "You're mean to Micha" or such vague statements as "You and Micha don't get along very well."

Next, ask the student what he or she has noticed about the problem. You'll learn a lot by garnering the student's perspective. If the student responds by saying, "Micha kicks me under the table" or even "Micha tells me to be quiet, too," you may suspect that there's more going on than was immediately apparent. On the other hand, "Micha's just so annoying" may point you toward thinking about this as a situation where one student is targeting another.

It's important not to make assumptions. Find out the facts from both children's point of view. If you suspect that one child is picking on another child in a way that is one-sided and mean, it's important to talk with each child separately. All too often, children who are being targeted say, "That's OK," when they're expected to state their point of view while sitting next to a child who has been systematically hurting them.

Children who bully often feel that what they're doing is just fine and they dive into blaming the target. Stick to the facts. If Troy is telling Micha to be quiet over and over, that's unacceptable behavior. "Micha is annoying" is not a reason to act mean toward her. Keep in mind that the most important goal is to preserve a classroom climate that is emotionally and physically safe for all children. There is no excuse that makes mean behavior acceptable. Whether or not Troy thinks that Micha uses a loud voice, contributes ideas to the group that don't make sense, or talks too much is not germane, even if Troy keeps bringing these opinions up in the discussion.

If you believe that you're dealing with a potential bullying situation, it's important to stop the behavior and give clear consequences. These consequences need to be matter-of-fact, nonpunitive, consistently applied to any child who engages in such behavior, and framed so as to protect the child who is targeted. You might, for example, say, "Telling one group member to be quiet is not respectful behavior. You will miss the next two group meetings and work independently. We'll talk again before you rejoin the group." When the child is ready to rejoin the group, remind him about the expectation for respectful behavior. Then, once the child rejoins the group, watch the group closely. If you see any hint of mean behavior, remove the child who is mistreating from that group permanently, placing him in a different group. It's important to protect the child who is being targeted. Often it takes close observation to detect such ongoing behavior.

In addition, follow the protocols that your school may have in place already for responding to bullying or behaviors that are gateways to bullying.

For more detailed information about intervening in gateway behaviors, see Chapter One.

Provide structures for taking turns within a small group

Learning how to listen respectfully and take turns talking in a small group can be especially challenging for children. If you notice that children are having trouble listening and responding respectfully with more than one other student, the first thing to do is to assess developmental readiness for small-group work. Students seven and younger will most likely not be successful working in small groups; partnering with just one classmate may be a better option for them. Even when children are developmentally ready to learn the skill of working in a small group, often around eight years old, listening and responding respectfully in a small group can be difficult. (For more about developmental considerations, see the text box on pages 113–115.)

Often children who can listen to one other child become confused and overwhelmed when there are multiple children in the group, all hoping to be heard. Children might use mean words and refuse to work with group members who feel troublesome to them. To deal with these challenges, children can benefit from learning structures that keep them firmly rooted in respectful practice. Below are two such structures.

Although these learning structures may seem a bit formulaic, they help children over bumpy spots in the road to learning respect for all. Once the bumps are navigated, children can grow into more natural ways to be together.

Use a "talking stick"

Many structures can help children take turns speaking when there's more than one other student waiting to be heard. One such structure is to use an object as a "talking stick"—children speak only when they have the object in their hand.

I first used this structure the year my classroom was wired with a sound system designed to help Vivian, a deaf child. I found that passing the microphone, a real-life necessity, brought order to the conversation during whole-class discussions. When we began working in small groups, the group that needed to use the microphone functioned smoothly, whereas other groups struggled with taking turns. So I introduced using objects such as a microphone, a puppet, a carved stick, and even a feather to the other groups and watched as their discussions became as orderly as the discussions in Vivian's group. After that, I used some form of talking stick whenever groups struggled with learning how to listen to each other.

Carefully teach how to use the talking stick. As with other structures, it's important to carefully teach children how to use a talking stick. Interactive Modeling lends itself to teaching this procedure. To introduce the talking stick, a teacher might begin by naming the ideal: "We all have things to say and we can learn from each other when we take turns speaking." As the teacher and then a student model passing the talking stick and speaking only when holding it, the class forms an image in their minds of what it looks like to use the talking stick to take turns. As everyone practices using the talking stick the teacher observes and coaches so she can reinforce when children are using the structure well and guide when they start to veer off course.

Supervise initial use of the talking stick. When children are ready to use the talking stick, have them do so as a whole group, under your supervision. Whole-class sharing time is a perfect opportunity for this first use of the talking stick. After one student shares some news, others raise their hands to respond with questions and comments. The sharer passes the stick to one of the potential responders. Students wait until they have the talking stick before they speak.

Once the class is comfortably following the rules for using the talking stick as a whole group, they're ready to use the structure for discussions in small groups. Be sure, however, to provide guidance by circulating, listening in, reinforcing, reminding and, when necessary, redirecting.

Use a "question, talk, talk, talk, question" format

Children can also learn to take turns in small groups by using a "question, talk, talk, talk, question" formula. I'm naming it this because that's how it would work in a group of four, an ideal group size. If you have groups of five it would be "question, talk, talk, talk, talk, question."

The first student in the small group asks an open-ended question. Going around the table, each of the other students responds with thoughts about the topic of the question. Then student number two asks a question and the others respond. This keeps going until everyone has had a chance to ask a question and hear group members' responses.

Here's what this format might look like in a third grade book club group. The students are reading *Charlotte's Web*. In preparation for the book club meeting, each student has written questions about the assigned chapter. Each holds a small card with the "question, talk, talk, talk, question" steps written on it. Erica asks, "If you were a pig and lost your only friend, how would you feel?" Each participant answers in turn. Suzanne talks about loneliness, Daniel about finding new friends, and Andrew about how he can't imagine being a pig, much less a lonely pig. Then

Suzanne asks her question, "Was Charlotte actually eager to be a pig's friend or was she just really patient?" The others reply in turn.

While the children meet in their book clubs, using "question, talk, talk, talk, question" their teacher circulates, listening in and reinforcing their use of the structure. She resists the temptation to join in with student literature discussions but rather sits back, observes, notices, and reinforces the children's positive interactions.

Plan a transition toward real conversations

Both the structures of "talking stick" and "question, talk, talk, talk, question" provide a step toward learning how to have a real conversation. When one person asks a question and each group member answers in turn, the discussion doesn't have the flow of a true conversation. It does, however, give children practice in taking turns and listening to each other's questions. Once the children have learned to take turns and listen to each other, you can plan a transition away from the formulaic conversation into a more nuanced and natural discussion.

Considerations About Child Development

Our goal in working on children's small-group and partnership skills is to foster a classroom atmosphere that feels safe and inclusive and prevents bullying. But if we force children outside their comfort zone, we'll undermine our efforts. Children's readiness to work in partnerships and small groups has a predictable developmental progression. Understanding this progression helps us decide when children are ready to learn a new group work skill and protects us and them from the frustration of reaching for a skill that they're not ready for. Following are some considerations about child development that can help you set up successful partner and group work situations. ▶

These guidelines are very general ones; the students you teach may develop at different rates. I offer these guidelines so that you can set goals for students that are realistic, developmentally speaking. I also offer them so that when something isn't working for the students, you can examine the situation through a developmental lens.

Kindergarten: If you teach kindergarten, your students may be happy to partner chat but might have very little recall of what their partner said. Experienced kindergarten teachers often listen in to partners and then make observations to the class about what the children said. "I heard several partners say that they noticed the rhymes in *Mrs. Wishy-Washy*," says Mrs. Hauer. "Rhymes help us read the words," she adds.

First grade: First graders, usually six years old, often beg to be allowed to work with partners. This is a highly social age. Nonetheless, to ensure success you'll need to teach such basics as how to hold the book, how to take turns speaking, or how to share materials with a partner.

Second grade: Second graders, most of whom are seven, tend to be private and self-absorbed. Putting these children in groups of four is often a frustrating experience for all involved, but they usually do well working alone or with just one other person. They thrive with restricted structures such as "talk, listen, talk, listen" written out for them to follow. First Jenine talks while Mikey listens, then Mikey talks while Jenine listens. Keeping their finger on the step they're doing will help each child remember when it's time to talk and when it's time to listen.

Third grade: Group work is the métier of most eight-year-olds, who make up the majority of third grade classes. With direct teaching about how to work in a group, eight-year-olds can manage smoothly in a group of four. Any group larger than that will most likely overwhelm them.

Fourth grade: By nine, children may become more individualistic and self-conscious, so it's particularly important in fourth grade to teach group structures meticulously and follow up with reinforcements and reminders. With careful teaching, fourth graders can work successfully in groups of four or five.

Fifth grade: Fifth graders, usually ten-year-olds, are commonly as willing and eager to work in groups as eight-year-olds. I've found that four is still the ideal group size, but most ten-year-olds can handle a group of up to six members if need be.

By fifth grade, many children are also beginning to define themselves by who their friends are. Left to themselves, they may choose to work only with classmates whom they think of as their friends, but they will work with everyone if you, the teacher, set the expectation that they work with all classmates in respectful and friendly ways. When we explain that they need to be "friendly" rather than "best friends," they will comply because "our teacher makes us." Using this simple excuse, they will learn to be respectful to all while still engaged in the developmentally appropriate task of making choices about friends.

For more about common child developmental characteristics in the classroom and their implications for teaching, see *Yardsticks: Children in the Classroom Ages 4–14*, 3rd edition, by Chip Wood, 2007, www.responsiveclassroom.org. ■

Communicating With Parents About Cooperative Learning Structures

As with other classroom structures you put in place, it's important to have open and clear communication with parents about how you organize partner and group work and how you introduce cooperative learning structures. Doing so will help reassure them that you are making every effort to ensure that this important part of their child's day is safe and productive.

Nonetheless, you may hear from parents about concerns they have, especially if you've worked on establishing good communication with them so that they feel comfortable talking with you. For example, concerned about her daughter's reading partner assignment, Laila's mother might call to say, "I hear that you partnered Marie with Laila for reading. They can't work together." Sometimes the reason is that Marie and Laila have joined up with different cliques in an undersupervised after-school activity. Sometimes it's that the families don't like each other. Often the parent is concerned about their child's safety with a particular partner. You want to preserve your relationship with the parents, you want to make sure that all of the students are safe, and you also want to preserve the class's sense of inclusion. What do you do?

Listen

It's important to listen to the adults in students' lives and hear what they have to say. They have information that you don't have. Once you've listened carefully, it's important to investigate and learn about the situation that parents describe. It's also important to reassure them that you will keep their child safe.

Investigate the situation

When Mrs. Safar, Laila's mother, explained to Laila's teacher, Mr. Reston, that Marie was calling Laila names at soccer practice, Mr. Reston investigated. He knew that he had to make sure that Marie wasn't bullying Laila. If that were the case, it would be dangerous to put Laila in a group with Marie.

He watched Marie and Laila work together in class. They listened to each other and made friendly comments. Knowing that children who are targeted are usually not able to assert their needs in front of the child doing the bullying, he had a private talk with Laila to try to understand what was going on. Laila assured him that both girls called each other names at soccer practice and that everyone on the team called everyone else names, too. Although Mr. Reston wasn't pleased to hear about the name-calling that prevailed at soccer practice, he was reassured about Laila and Marie's relationship.

In another classroom, Mrs. McEntyre received a call from Mr. Hall, who explained that his son, Wayne, couldn't work with his classmate Danielle because their families didn't like each other, so Mr. Hall was afraid that Danielle might be mean to Wayne. Mrs. McEntyre said that she would watch the two students carefully. She observed and noticed that Wayne and Danielle worked together respectfully and even joyfully in school. Based on these observations, she felt that Wayne and Danielle were appropriate work partners.

Intervene if you discover any unkind behaviors

Sometimes, of course, parents' calls will alert you to situations that need an intervention. If either teacher described above suspected bullying behavior, the teacher would stop the bullying behavior and make sure the children did not work in the same group. It's important, at all costs, to make sure that the child who is being targeted is not left to work alone due to the separation. Children who are being targeted with bullying behavior need the social support of the classroom community, rather than isolation.

Respectfully communicate your decision to parents

Once you know that the students are treating each other respectfully, preserve the inclusive atmosphere in the classroom by letting parents know that the children will continue to work together. Explain why you are keeping them together and reassure the children's parents that you will supervise their children closely and that you will make sure their children are safe in the classroom.

Mr. Reston decided that although Laila and Marie might treat each other disrespectfully on a chaotic-sounding soccer team, in the positive climate of this classroom they read together in a supportive manner. He called Mrs. Safar to explain this to her. Mr. Reston thanked Mrs. Safar for bringing the situation to his attention and assured her that it was important to him that Laila be safe in school. He described his observation of the two reading partners, focusing on such specifics as the way Laila and Marie listened to each other carefully, laughed, and smiled as they read together. He encouraged Mrs. Safar to call him again if Laila reported any unkind treatment in school.

Mr. Reston also told Mrs. Safar that both girls had reported that "Everyone calls each other names on the soccer team." He asked Mrs. Safar if she had noticed this and encouraged her to discuss this behavior with the girls' coach. The fact that Mr. Reston seemed concerned about Laila's life outside of school helped to build a bond between him and Mrs. Safar.

Wayne's teacher called Mr. Hall to explain that Wayne and Danielle worked together smoothly in school. She described enough specific details to reassure Mr. Hall that it would be safe for Wayne and Danielle to remain partners for the time being.

Plan opportunities for parents to experience their child's classroom community

Parents may base their mental image of their child's classroom on a less-than-safe classroom from their own childhood, unfriendly interactions they may have seen between children outside of school, or the way classrooms are portrayed in TV shows with sarcastic comments punctuated by the laugh track. Once the classroom community is friendly and inclusive, invite parents in to see and feel the climate of kindness.

Some teachers invite parents in to serve as classroom helpers. Others invite parents to join in classroom activities. You could invite parents in for a Morning Meeting if you hold these, for writing workshop, for a math games period, or for any other time of day when you can showcase the way students work together respectfully. Parents' anxiety is often assuaged when they have a mental image of the way the classroom actually is.

K e y   I d e a s

Cooperative learning structures provide an important way for children to get to know each other and learn to treat each other respectfully.

For cooperative learning structures to be effective, children need explicit teaching of respectful work skills such as listening carefully, taking turns, and sharing materials.

The first step is to observe children at work so that you can identify any deficits in their skills.

Interactive Modeling, role-playing, and the fishbowl format are useful strategies for teaching positive group skills.

Naming the ideal for students reinforces the importance of behaving in safe and inclusive ways.

Anchor charts provide useful reminders of newly learned skills.

Provide coaching for individuals or small groups that are struggling with newly learned skills.

Provide structures to help students learn how to take turns in small groups. Two such structures are using a "talking stick" and using the "question, talk, talk, talk, question" format.

Pay attention to developmental considerations as you plan cooperative structures.

Plan groupings carefully so that no child is placed in a group that could feel unsafe.

Remove the child who is doing the bullying rather than the child who is targeted if you suspect that bullying behavior is occurring in a group.

Listen carefully to parents' concerns about children's small-group work arrangements, investigate, and follow up with parents.

Chapter Five

Outside of the Classroom

. . .

Sandy and Miranda appeared to be close friends. They played together at recess, sat together at lunch, and talked about visits to each other's homes. However, at lunch every single day Sandy insisted that Miranda give up her dessert. And every day, Miranda, confused and frightened, turned over her fruit or her cup of pudding to Sandy.

Jake seemed like a solid member of the classroom community. He worked smoothly with other students and was friendly to all. Nonetheless, Jake was alone every day at recess—and not by choice. If he tried to join a team game on the playground, no one picked him. If he tried to join the line-up when kids were shooting baskets, others turned their backs.

Remember Paul from the introduction to this book? From kindergarten well into middle school, he was targeted by children engaging in overt bullying behavior on the school bus. Mean words led to exclusion and physical assaults. But despite the severity and duration of the bullying, his parents and classroom teachers were not aware of what was going on.

Bullying and the mean behavior that leads to bullying often take place in the more lightly supervised areas of school: the halls, the playground, the cafeteria, and the school bus. In addition, children often don't report to adults incidences of mean behavior that occur in those areas. Miranda, Jake, and Paul were each part of a cooperative classroom community that emphasized safety and inclusiveness. However, once they and their classmates moved out of the classroom and away from the supports that kept their communities kind and caring, these students were no longer safe.

Collaborating With Grade-Level Colleagues

In many cases, you can put the ideas I present in this chapter into action on your own, but in some cases, I suggest working with a grade-level team. Whether you use a brief portion of team meetings to strategize with colleagues or informal moments such as lunchtime in the teachers' room, it's helpful if you and your teammates can work together in your bullying prevention efforts. That's because when children move out of the classroom, they are often moving into settings that include other children from their grade level, and in all likelihood some percentage of children from that grade level will be involved in any mean behaviors taking place.

Their peers tested the limits and discovered that they had free rein to try out mean behaviors. When these behaviors were not stopped, they escalated.

What can classroom teachers do about this problem? The optimal approach is to connect classroom teaching to a comprehensive schoolwide bullying prevention plan. But even if a school or district doesn't have such a plan, classroom teachers can do a lot—on their own or in collaboration with grade-level colleagues—to help students use the social skills that they're learning in the classroom as they move into settings that require more independence.

Specifically, in this chapter you'll learn about the following:

- Keeping a close eye on areas outside the classroom

- Taking classroom rules outside the classroom

- Using modeling and role-playing to help students practice safe and inclusive behaviors outside the classroom

- Giving students reminders and reinforcements for outside-the-classroom behaviors

- Providing structures that enhance inclusiveness outside the classroom

- Collaborating with colleagues who supervise outside-the-classroom areas

Keeping a Close Eye on Areas Outside the Classroom

In previous chapters, I've discussed the role of close observation within the classroom. Observing students outside the classroom is equally valuable. Through close observation, you can learn about students' kind behaviors as well as their unkind behaviors. You learn who is "in" and who is "out," and you can notice those small mean behaviors that are gateways to bullying. This knowledge is essential to preventing bullying.

Admittedly, outside-the-classroom observation is sometimes hard to fit into a busy day, especially when you're not scheduled for lunchroom, hall, or recess duty. However, even a few minutes observing the lunchroom or the hall can yield a tremendous amount of information. When you *are* scheduled for recess, hall, or lunchroom duty, you can use that time effectively to observe students and learn about their lives outside the classroom.

Research supports the need for this increased vigilance. For example, there is extensive evidence that a great deal of the bullying behavior that happens on the playground is not noticed by the adults in charge. Wendy Craig and Debra Pepler videotaped recess in their classic study of children's interactions mentioned in the introduction to this book. They observed frequent bullying incidents with minimal adult intervention. However, most of these same adults reported that they "nearly always" intervened in bullying incidents. In one interaction, two children march another child, hands held behind her back, across the playground, ordering her to "Kiss the tree," while a teacher stands obliviously nearby (Craig & Pepler, 1998).

It's easy to see how things like this can happen. I know from my own experience that it's not always clear what role classroom teachers ought to be playing during our stint at recess duty. Because of this lack of clarity, it's easy to fall into visiting with colleagues and treating recess duty as a much needed break. This stance means that there's lots of space for mean behavior to emerge.

The same thing can happen in the lunchroom. Teachers often pass through the cafeteria briefly if at all, dropping students off before hurrying off to make copies, return phone calls, and eat their own lunches.

You can play a different role. As you work on bullying prevention strategies with the children, I encourage you to do some detective work—either on your own or with grade-level colleagues—to discover what children's lives are like in the areas outside the classroom. Following are some ideas for how to do this.

When you are on duty

If you are assigned to lunch, recess, or hall duties, you can spend some of the time closely observing student interaction. Here are some things to look for:

- **On the playground, who decides on the teams for group games?** Is it the same children consistently? Do they carefully select a "cool" team and a team of "losers"? This can set the stage for bullying behavior.

- **Who plays with whom on the playground or sits with whom in the lunchroom?** Cliques that may remain underground within the structure of the classroom become evident when children choose where to sit in the lunchroom or whom to play with at recess. You may see children running to their lunch seats, saving seats for some and pushing others away. You may, if you listen for it, hear name-calling between groups. You may, on the other hand, see groups of friends who are inclusive toward others. You may see welcoming expressions and hear friendly words. Exclusive cliques can set the tone for bullying. Inclusive friendships can set a tone of community and caring.

- **Who sits alone in the lunchroom or relies on chatting with the teachers at recess?** When I started to closely observe students during my recess duty, I noticed that Jake, who I had believed to be fully a part of the social life of the class, wandered the playground alone. Without the inclusive structures I'd put in place in the classroom,

Jake's social isolation became apparent. The same thing can happen in the lunchroom. This is a serious problem because there is ample evidence that social isolation is connected to children's being targeted (Buhs, Ladd, & Herald-Brown, 2010).

■ **On the playground, watch children's body language.** Are some children always the chasers or do they switch roles? When the first graders run outside to play, Mark shouts, "Let's play tag—Jamie's 'It.'" Jamie is always "It" and he stays "It" throughout the game, a not-so-subtle form of picking on Jamie that can quickly escalate to even more aggressive forms of targeting him.

What is the posture and affect of children who walk the playground alone? My student Becca walked the perimeter of the playground by herself. Her body was relaxed, her face calm. When I asked her if she'd like someone to play with, she replied, "No, I've been with people all morning; I need to be by myself now." Becca was fine— she simply needed the respite of some time alone.

Pete, on the other hand, stood outside the basketball game with his head down, feet shuffling, looking as though he longed to be included. When I asked him if he'd tried to join the game he said, "They told me I'm a loser and I can't play." This type of exclusion is a step along the continuum toward bullying.

■ **Who is laughing and who looks fearful or unhappy?** Oftentimes, children's facial expressions and body language let us know whether one child is teetering on the verge of bullying the other or whether they're just playing together.

The school day is over, the busses are being called. Ms. Meyer stands in the hallway supervising as children make their way to the busses. Eric and Frankie bump into each other rhythmically as they move down the hall. As Eric bumps Frankie, Frankie laughs uproariously. Frankie then gives Eric a bump and Eric grins. These two are having fun, bonding and releasing tension after an afternoon of too much sitting still.

Meanwhile, Elena and Kim walk down the hall together. Kim reaches out her hand and tickles Elena. One might think that this is a benign and friendly gesture, but Elena cringes, her mouth turns down slightly, and her eyes turn away from Kim. This unwelcome gesture may be a gateway to bullying, a warning that things are going to heat up on the way home.

Ms. Meyer ignores Frankie and Eric's playful behavior. However, she stops Kim and says, "That doesn't look friendly to me." She also makes a mental note to tell Kim and Elena's teacher, Mr. Richardson, about the behaviors that she saw so that he can follow up with some careful observation of the girls' relationship.

When you aren't on duty

There are lots of ways to learn about children's lives outside of the classroom even if you're not spending an entire recess on the playground or an entire dismissal time in the hall. Brief observations can reveal more information than you might imagine.

Besides keeping children safe everywhere in school, another reason to make the time for these brief observations, even if you're not on duty, is that the mean behaviors that go on outside the classroom have an impact on classroom life. For example, the child who is worried about being targeted on the playground will be preoccupied with thoughts about recess today and what recess will be like tomorrow—and this preoccupation can interfere with the ability to concentrate on academics.

Following are some ideas for how to fit brief outside-the-classroom observations into a busy teaching day.

Accompany children to the cafeteria and the playground

Even if you aren't assigned to cafeteria duty, recess duty, or hall duty, occasional brief observations in these areas can be enlightening. When you walk your class to recess, spend a few extra minutes on the playground, watching the children sort themselves out into play groups. Who plays with whom? Who is accepted? Who is rejected? If you pick students up at the end of recess, plan to occasionally arrive a few minutes early. Notice some of these same interactions.

If you pick students up in the cafeteria, arrive early on occasion. Or if you drop students off, spend a few minutes watching as they get settled. Who sits with whom? How are they treating each other? Use these and the other observation questions that I suggested in the "When you are on duty" section to assess what you're seeing.

Observe children as they enter the classroom from recess, lunch, or the bus

Listening to children's conversations with each other and paying close attention to things they say to us about the time that they spend outside the classroom are seemingly obvious yet often neglected tools that we can use to gain insight into children's experiences outside their classrooms.

Jessica, Annie, and Gretel, who all ride bus 7, arrive together. Jessica and Annie have their arms wrapped around each other's shoulders. Gretel follows behind, her head down, eyes on the floor and feet dragging. You can guess that something has gone wrong on bus 7 and make a mental note to keep an eye on how things are going among the three girls.

Listening can also help you identify recurrent problems. As children tumble in from recess, teachers often hear "That wasn't fair" or "They wouldn't play with me." Although these might seem like small complaints that don't warrant intervention, when you hear the same complaint day after day, it's time to investigate. Do children complain about certain games? Perhaps the game that is accompanied by complaints of unfairness needs more supervision.

Notice patterns in children's behavior around outside-the-classroom times

You can also notice patterns in children's behavior: Who's on time to school and who's regularly tardy? Who tries to get to the end of the line when the class lines up to leave the room? These behavior patterns offer hints to follow up on.

When Alexis was consistently late for school, I called her mother. "She doesn't want to ride the school bus so she keeps missing it," her mother explained. Upon further investigation, I learned that Alexis was being mistreated by a group of older girls on the school bus. I spoke to the teacher of the children engaging in the mean behavior. Their teacher had a serious talk with them. Things calmed right down once they knew that their teacher was "on to" their school bus behaviors.

Pay attention to behavior patterns around recess. Would certain children rather stay inside and "help you out" than go to recess? Do some children consistently "forget" their homework and then offer to finish it during recess time? Those children may, unknown to you, be targets of bullying behaviors on the playground.

The same pattern can emerge around the lunchroom. Do you have a student who needs to go to the nurse every day right before lunch? Perhaps the lunchroom is feeling unsafe for that child.

Talk with children about their experiences outside the classroom

In addition to informally listening to what children have to say, you can structure ways for them to reflect on their experiences outside the classroom. One of the areas that teachers have little access to is the school bus. Taking the time to reflect with students about life on the bus can yield information that you can act on, despite the fact that you're not physically on the bus.

As the kindergarten students arrive on Monday morning, Mr. Rinaldi has them draw pictures of themselves on the school bus for their morning work. Mr. Wright assigns a journal reflection for his sixth graders about how children are treating each other on the bus. Later on in the day, both groups of students spend a few minutes sharing their reflections. The emphasis is on the children's thoughts and feelings. "When do you feel welcome on the bus?" asks Mr. Rinaldi. "What might you do to be a leader on your bus and help younger children feel welcome?" asks Mr. Wright.

You can also reflect with children about areas in the school that you have some access to, which can richly complement the information that you glean by observing. "How are things going in the lunchroom? What is friendly about the lunchroom? What feels unfriendly about the lunchroom?" asks a written message from Ms. Taylor as fourth graders enter their classroom. Later on, as part of the daily Morning Meeting, the children discuss times when they feel included in the lunchroom and times they feel excluded. Ms. Taylor is gathering information that will help her ensure safety in the lunchroom.

Use a survey with the children to identify safe and unsafe areas

Evidence-based bullying prevention programs often recommend surveying students to discover where they feel safe and where they feel unsafe in school (Olweus et al., 2007). These surveys usually offer a definition of bullying and then ask children if they have experienced or seen behavior that fits the definition happening in a variety of specific spots such as the lunchroom, the playground, the halls, the bathrooms, and the school bus. With the resulting information, schools can increase supervision in areas where children feel unsafe. Such surveys have been used with children as young as eight years old but are more commonly used with children who are ten and older.

You can survey just the children you teach or work with grade-level colleagues to survey all children at your grade level. In Chapter Six, you'll find information about creating a survey, including sample questions you could include.

Although surveys are generally not used with children younger than eight, there are ways to gather information from young children. Ms. Pelis has prepared a chart for her first graders to respond to. At the top she has written "Safe" with a smiley face and "Unsafe" with a frowny face. She's created a box on the chart for each of a variety of areas in the school such as playground, lunchroom, school bus, bathroom, and hall. As the students arrive she carefully guides them to draw smiley faces in the boxes for the areas where they feel safe at school, frowny faces for where they feel unsafe. Many of her students place frowny faces in the "playground" box.

Down the hall in Mr. Oakley's second grade, the children are working on mapping skills as part of their social studies curriculum. First, the whole class creates a map of the school. Then Mr. Oakley adds a bullying prevention component to the lesson. He asks children if there are places in school where they feel unsafe. If they feel unsafe somewhere, he asks them to place a red adhesive dot on that spot. Mr. Oakley is surprised to see that many children in the class put a red dot on the second grade bathrooms, down the hall from their classroom.

Once you gather information from children, it's important to follow up with investigations and other steps needed. For example, students in Ms. Pelis's first grade classroom discuss their chart about playground concerns later in the day. The class has just recently completed a bullying prevention lesson where the children have learned to "report to a responsible adult" if they feel that they are being targeted (see primary grades Lesson Three in Chapter Six). Ms. Pelis realizes during the discussion that the children are not sure who that responsible adult would be on the playground. The class makes a list of who they might report to. Ms. Pelis makes a note to herself to talk with these adults so that they will be ready to take action when the children report to them.

Meanwhile, the second graders in Mr. Oakley's class sit on the rug and discuss the second grade bathrooms. "The fifth graders use our bathroom if they need to go during lunch," declares Maurice. "When they see us in there they call us 'little twerps' and say they're going to stuff us in the toilet." Later on in the day Mr. Oakley discusses the bathroom situation with his principal. His principal will work with the fifth grade team around building kind behaviors toward younger children. He also decides to reconfigure the fifth grade lunchroom arrangement so that fifth graders use a different bathroom during lunch.

Taking Classroom Rules Outside the Classroom

Rules that guide behavior are essential to creating a safe environment throughout the school, not just in the classroom. Some schools establish whole-school rules that serve this function; such rules are a key component in a schoolwide bullying prevention effort. But even if you don't have schoolwide rules, you can teach students that "our rules go with us," right down to having a student representative carry a copy of classroom rules and posting these rules in the cafeteria, specials classrooms, and other spaces the class goes to.

However, it's not enough to simply carry the rules from place to place. It's essential to spend time discussing what abiding by the rules will look like and sound like in those places to help children pay attention to the rules in a variety of specific situations.

Classroom rules can help make recess safer

Bullying at school often begins on the playground. A good starting point for teaching about safe and kind recess behavior is to reflect with students about how classroom rules apply to recess. Questions such as "How does our rule to respect each other apply to games of tag during recess?" or "What would it look like and sound like to be kind to classmates during recess today?" can help students think more concretely about how to put their broad rules into action.

It's beneficial to collaborate with grade-level colleagues around recess issues. Although individual teachers can have fruitful discussions about specific applications of the rules, coordinating with teachers whose students are out on the playground with your students can yield even better results because all the students will then be operating from the same set of expectations.

A third grade team applies classroom rules to the playground

One year the third grade students at my school fell into playing a violent and hierarchical version of football at recess. Football became a way that socially powerful children intimidated less powerful children.

I knew that I needed to address this problem—and that I needed to coordinate my efforts with the other third grade teachers, since it wasn't just students from my classroom playing these rough games. We decided to each talk with our students.

In my class, we reflected on how the classroom rules to "be safe" and "be kind" would help us know what to do during football. What would kind behavior look like and sound like as students divided into teams, played football, and congratulated each other at the end of the game?

The children devised some rules that would support safe and kind behavior during their football games and posted them right by the door to the playground. As they lined up for recess, they took turns reading these student-generated rules aloud:

- A teacher must supervise the football game.

- Teams will be chosen by counting off.

- Players will pass to everyone.

- Quarterbacks will rotate.

- Touch only.

When they returned from recess each day, they evaluated themselves, reflecting on how they'd done at following the football rules. I used simple structures for the reflection, for example, saying, "Hold up fingers, one through five, to show how you did at following our football rules today." The vast majority of the children who played football held up four or five fingers. I certainly wasn't expecting perfection at this challenge—four fingers was a huge improvement over their past behavior.

In addition, the teachers on recess duty took responsibility for stopping the game if it degenerated, and they made a point of letting the child's classroom teacher know if one child spiraled out of control. Recess safety improved immeasurably.

Early in the year, talk with children about how classroom rules apply to lunchroom behavior

Taking the time at the beginning of the year to talk about how classroom rules can guide lunchtime behavior can save you from spending hours trying to solve the inevitable problems that will crop up if you don't have such talks.

Early in the year, Mr. Gonzales discusses with students how the classroom rules apply to the cafeteria. "If our rule is to be kind," he says, "how can we be kind in the cafeteria?" Children's responses are as simple as "We can help someone who drops his tray" and as sophisticated as "We can make sure that everyone has someone to sit with."

Mr. Gonzales then checks in with students after lunch to see how they did with being kind. "Think to yourself about how you did at following our rule to be kind during lunch today," he says. He then asks them to think of a goal for the next day: "What's one thing you can do tomorrow to make lunch more friendly?"

Structuring reflections

The discussions that Mr. Gonzales had with the children helped them feel invested in the classroom rules. Discussions such as these are valuable at the beginning of the year, when children are first learning about behavior expectations, and throughout the year, when new and challenging situations arise.

Following are some guidelines for structuring and facilitating these discussions.

Help children remember the purpose of rules

First, prompt the children to remember their relationship to the rules. "We created rules to help us keep our classroom safe and friendly" or "Our rules help us to have a safe and friendly classroom" are statements that remind children about the purpose of the rules.

Frame the challenges in positive terms

Second, bring up possible outside-the-classroom challenges while keeping your language positive. Keep the focus on what we *do* want (safety outside the classroom) rather than what we don't want ("We will not be mean").

To stimulate this discussion, it's helpful to use open-ended questions—questions that have multiple possible answers. Here are some possibilities:

- How can we keep the cafeteria as friendly as our classroom is?

- How can we make sure everyone's feelings are safe on the playground?

- What might you do if you see someone alone on the playground (or in the lunchroom)?

- How can we make sure that everyone who wants to play has the chance to play?

- How can we make the school bus feel safe in the way our classroom feels safe?

- (For older children) How can you be a leader and take care of the younger children on the school bus?

Gather students' ideas

Next, collect student ideas while keeping the discussion focused on what they *do* want. Students can be highly invested in their hopes for friendliness and safety, whereas they're not likely to be invested in a list of prohibitions. For example, if a child says, "We shouldn't throw stuff on the school bus," a teacher might say, "If you aren't going to throw things, what *will* you do?"

It's often helpful to use a T-chart, a two-column chart with "What will it look like?" at the top of one column and "What will it sound like?" at the top of the other. The T-chart can stay up in the classroom for a while or it can be stored in a convenient spot and brought out when the challenging time (recess, lunch, independent hall walking) is about to begin.

Young children often enjoy drawing pictures to remind themselves what safe and careful outside-the-classroom behavior will look like and sound like. The act of creating posters and pictures cements the learning for the students, and the visuals can serve as a strong reminder of positive behaviors.

Quick conversations can have a positive impact

In addition to in-depth discussions of rules, you can also have quick, in-the-moment conversations about behavior expectations outside the classroom. Ms. Gilbert's fourth graders are lined up at the door, ready to go to lunch. Today, their lunch period overlaps the first grade lunch period. Ms. Gilbert says, "One of our rules says to respect each other. How can you show respect to others today at lunch?" Several hands go up and children respond, "Be kind to the younger kids," "Say 'Hi' to kids in other classes," "Don't bump people." "If you're not going to bump people, what will you do?" Ms. Gilbert prompts. "Watch where you're going and keep your body in your own space," a child replies. "Sounds like you're ready for the cafeteria," Ms. Gilbert says, and the children head out the door.

A quick conversation at the end of the day can help keep expectations of kind and safe behavior alive for children as they ride the bus home. The fourth graders in Ms. Nelson's class are packed up and ready to go home. They sit in a circle. "Our school rule says to be kind," says Ms. Nelson. "How might that rule apply to the bus ride home?" she asks. The children think for a minute and then hands go up. "I could sit with Jenny," offers Sarah. "She just moved into our neighborhood and doesn't know many kids yet." Other children nod in agreement.

Strategy in Action:
A Fifth Grade Team Creates Playground Rules

One spring, as part of their bullying prevention efforts, a fifth grade team administered a questionnaire to all of the fifth grade students. Children responded to questions about where in school they felt safe and where in school they had experienced behaviors defined by the questionnaire as "bullying," such as being hit, pushed, kicked, teased, called names, or purposely excluded. To their teachers' surprise, one quarter of the children surveyed reported experiencing "bullying" on the playground during the past month. The fifth grade team could see that they needed to improve safety on the playground.

First, they gathered information

The classroom teachers, each in turn during their recess duty, spent a week noticing closely. They followed pairs who hid behind trees, really listened to the play under the play structure, and noticed the body language and facial expressions of children chasing each other. They also discussed playground safety with the recess paraprofessionals. As might happen to a lot of us when we first actively observe outside-the-classroom behavior, what they saw surprised and alarmed them.

Many of the boys who played on the high-status travel soccer team played soccer every day. They took charge of choosing teams and excluded children who were less skilled at the game.

Students who weren't playing soccer didn't have a whole lot to do. Many girls gathered in small groups and whispered about each other, hiding behind the play structure and jumping out to make mean comments as girls in other groups walked by.

Four children grabbed the swings each day and monopolized them. This group engaged in lots of unsafe behavior, such as getting the swings going really high and then jumping off, twisting the swings and flinging them at neighboring swingers, and so on. When other children tried to get a swing the swingers loudly chanted, "We own the swings."

One small group of children spent recess throwing rocks at grade mates.

The information that the teachers discovered provided a wake-up call. When they sat down to talk and began to list the behaviors that they had seen, they realized they needed to take immediate action.

They intervened quickly to stop the misbehaviors

Some of the more dangerous misbehaviors needed to be stopped right away. The teachers, in discussion with the recess paraprofessionals, decided to tape off the swing area until they could establish expectations of physical and emotional safety on the swings. As the children lined up for recess, the lead recess teacher explained to all of the children in the grade level that swings were off limits until everyone decided together how to make them safe. They also announced that any behavior that hurt children's bodies (or any attempts to hurt children's bodies) would lead to separation from other children at recess for the day. The adults supervised recess behavior closely. The first time a child picked up a rock and started to fling it, they honored their words by following through. That child was immediately separated from the other children.

Next, they established clear rules

At their next grade-level meeting, the fifth grade teachers looked at all their classroom rules, identified which ones related to recess, and consolidated them to make a few simple recess rules:

- We will be safe
- We will be fair
- We will include everyone

They discussed their plan with the fifth grade recess paraprofessionals and explained how they hoped to improve supervision. Needless to say, the paraprofessionals were delighted by the support. ▶

They presented the rules to the students

Back in their own classrooms, the teachers presented the rules to the students. Each teacher explained that they had noticed that recess had become unsafe. They shared the "recess rules," explaining that they were derived from their own classroom rules which the children had helped to create. They brainstormed with their students what the rules might look like and sound like on the playground.

The children had a lot to say. "We'll need to share the swings if we're going to include everyone," said Kevin, who often was the "king of the swings." Jeff said, "I guess the teachers will choose the soccer teams now if we're going to include everyone." Maxine said, "If recess is going to be safe, some kids are going to have to stop saying mean things."

They continued to reflect with the students about how the rules applied to playground behavior

In the following days, each teacher devoted brief periods of time each day to reflection with the students about what their recess rules "be safe," "be fair," and "include everyone" would look like and sound like on the playground. As the children lined up for recess, Mr. Roland asked, "What might you do today to include everyone on the playground?"

When the children returned from recess, Ms. Young asked, "Think about how you did today at being safe. Chat with the person next to you in line about something you did to be safe or something safe that you saw a classmate do." Ms. Young listened in while her students chatted with partners. "It sounds like everyone shared the swings," she said.

In the following days, each teacher continued his or her careful observations and interventions. When Mindy clung to Fiona's neck and Fiona, with a distressed expression, said repeatedly, "Stop it, stop it," Ms. Young stepped right in. "Mindy, that's not safe. Play over here by yourself for the rest of recess."

The tone of the playground became much more positive. Children laughed, chatted sociably, and enjoyed themselves. The teachers' interventions had made recess safer. ■

Using Modeling and Role-Playing to Help Students Practice Safe and Inclusive Behaviors

Discussing how the rules apply to all areas of the school is an important first step, but children need opportunities to actually practice safe and inclusive behavior. The *Responsive Classroom* strategies of Interactive Modeling and role-playing help children do this. (See Chapter Four for detailed information about both strategies.)

Use modeling to review and practice specific procedures

The *Responsive Classroom* strategy of Interactive Modeling can be used to help children practice specific procedures that will maintain order and minimize opportunities for mean behavior. For example, you can use modeling to teach how to listen respectfully to a lunch buddy or how to sit safely, child's back to seat back and child's bottom to seat bottom, on the school bus. Modeling is also a way to teach safe and careful tagging at a recess tag game or safe standing or sitting in line while children wait to go home on their school busses.

Early in the year at Kensington Avenue School in Springfield, Massachusetts, teachers use Interactive Modeling to review lunchroom protocols such as lining up, getting a lunch, using appropriate voice levels, and sitting at the correct table. When students are asked to demonstrate the appropriate behaviors themselves and notice how their classmates demonstrate these expected behaviors, the behaviors become lodged in their memory and they're more likely to use the behaviors when the time comes. Interactive Modeling is a key reason that the lunchroom behavior at Kensington is safe, orderly, and inclusive.

Meanwhile, to model safe sitting on the school bus, first grade teacher Ms. Guerin lines up chairs in the front of the classroom, mimicking school bus seats. "We're going to practice how to sit safely on the bus," she explains to the children. Ms. Guerin sits on one of the chairs. "What do you notice about how I'm sitting?" she asks. "Your feet are on the floor," says Mark.

"Your back is against the back of the chair," says Lucy. "Your bottom is on the seat of the chair," says Malik. "To be safe on the school bus, you'll sit back to seat back, bottom to seat bottom," Ms. Guerin explains. "Who else would like to show us what this looks like?" Eager hands go up and Ms. Guerin gives everyone in the class a chance to practice.

As the children line up for the bus, Ms. Guerin reminds them, "Remember, to be safe, back-to-back, bottom-to-bottom." When the children's bodies are in their seats, opportunities to engage in mean behaviors are diminished.

Use role-playing to help children prepare for potentially tricky situations

Role-playing is a strategy to help children explore a range of responses to potentially tricky situations. As you observe a specific group of students in the lunchroom or on the playground or hear about their struggles on the school bus, you can learn which challenges they're facing as they practice taking care of their own needs as well as the needs of those around them. Challenges that might benefit from role-playing include:

- What to do if you notice a classmate alone on the playground every day

- How to ask to join a game on the playground

- How to share the jump ropes or other equipment on the playground so that it's fair and fun for everyone

- How to invite someone to eat lunch with you

- What to do if two students want to sit next to the same person at lunch

- What you might talk about when you sit with a lunch partner

- What you might do to keep yourself busy while allowing the bus driver to do her job safely on the bus ride home

- How you might help younger children feel safe on the school bus

For example, fourth grade teacher Mrs. Jones has noticed that students have been struggling with where to sit at lunch. One girl, in particular, seems to be a desired lunch partner. As soon as Anna sits down, several other children vie for the spot next to her. Mrs. Jones knows that this situation has the potential for mean and exclusive behavior.

She gathers students in a circle. "Today we're going to do a role-play to help us think and practice how to decide who sits where in the lunchroom. Our rules say to include everyone. How can we do that when several people want to sit in the same spot?" The students nod knowingly. They are interested. This is a problem that they're all well aware of.

"Pretend I'm a student," she says. "We're going into the lunchroom and I really want to sit near my friend, Denise. I know that Mary and Paulina want to sit near Denise, too. What might I do to include everyone and take care of my own wishes to be with my friends?" Mrs. Jones has created fictional names to keep the role-play at a slight remove from the actual classroom struggle.

Mrs. Jones collects ideas and writes them on a flip chart:

"You could talk with Denise, Mary, and Paulina and make a plan so that you can all sit together without arguing about the seat next to Denise."

"You could sit in partners, Denise and Mary, you and Paulina, and then switch another day."

"You could try sitting with someone else. We have lots of nice kids in our class."

Mrs. Jones tries out one of the ideas. "OK, I'm going to try one idea while Suzette, Stacy, and Janet play the roles of Denise, Mary, and Paulina."

She goes up to the other players. "I have an idea," she says. "I think lunch might be more fun for all of us if we sat with some other kids in our class and not only with each other. Let's see if we can get some other kids to join us."

Mrs. Jones says, "Stop," and the class discusses what they noticed. They comment that the girls might indeed have more fun if they sit with more people.

The class continues to act out some of the ideas on the chart and debrief about what they noticed.

The next day Mrs. Jones notices that the girls who normally all rushed to one seat have planned ahead about who would sit in the coveted spot. When she picks up the students after lunch she notices a large group of children sitting at the table where Anna is sitting, everyone appearing to enjoy themselves.

Giving Students Reminders and Reinforcements

Once teachers have introduced strategies for making the areas outside the classroom safe and friendly and children have had opportunities to practice these strategies under supervision, teachers can use reminding and reinforcing language to help children continue these behaviors.

Reminders prompt children to remember the established behavior expectations. For example, after teaching safe sitting on the bus, remind children as they leave the classroom, "Remember, back-to-back and bottom-to-bottom." You can also ask children to do this reminding. For example, as the children line up to go outside, ask, "Who can remind us which strategies we came up with yesterday for making sure that everyone has someone to play with?"

Reinforcements acknowledge and name children's attempts at positive behavior. For example, as the children arrive in the morning, a teacher might say to the class, "I'm noticing friendly conversation as you walk down the hall" or, to an individual who has been less than inclusive in the past, "I saw that you were friendly with all of the girls who have lockers near yours."

Here are some tips for using reinforcing and reminding language effectively:

- Keep your language positive, reminding children of the class's vision of a caring community.

- Remind children about behaviors that you have already taught rather than reminding about behaviors that you assume they should know.

- Use reinforcing language to support children's actual positive behaviors rather than pretending they're doing something that they're not.

- Reinforce individuals privately rather than using your public observations of one child's successes to manipulate other children into behaving well.

For more information about reinforcing and reminding language, see *The Power of Our Words: Teacher Language That Helps Children Learn* by Paula Denton, EdD, 2007, www.responsiveclassroom.org.

> ### Some Language to Try
>
> *Remember, back to seat back and bottom to seat bottom.*
>
> *Who can remind us . . . ?*
>
> *I hear friendly conversations.*
>
> *You were friendly to everyone in your group.*

Providing Structures That Enhance Inclusiveness

Sometimes children need specific structures to ensure inclusiveness and safety at recess, in the lunchroom, and on the bus. Depending on the developmental level of the children you teach and the time of year, you may decide to set up a format that minimizes choice and maximizes equitable treatment for all. Assigned seating in the cafeteria, for example, guarantees that everyone will have someone to sit with. Following are some ideas for providing structure to increase inclusiveness at recess, in the lunchroom, and on the bus.

Provide structures at recess that include everyone

You and your colleagues may have observed rough or excluding behavior on the playground. Perhaps students have reported that the playground is a spot in school where they feel unsafe. If so, you can plan structures that will increase inclusiveness and safety.

Structure selection for team sports

Choosing teams for team sports is an area where exclusion often flourishes. If this is the case in your school or grade level, you might decide, in collaboration with others who supervise recess, to use a structure for forming teams. You could group the children who plan to play a particular game and have them count off (one, two, one, two) to select teams. You could pass out numbered Popsicle sticks, with those drawing odd numbers on one team and those drawing even numbers on the other.

Whatever method you use, it's important to discuss it with the children first, making sure that they understand how such team selection structures connect with classroom rules and support a positive vision for life in school. To avoid arguments about team selection methods, children also need to know which method will be used on a particular day.

Sometimes it's helpful to stop team sports for a period of time (a few days to a week) and then reopen the sports with a new structure, which you've carefully introduced. That way you'll have a fresh start with a fresh way to make sure that everyone is taken care of.

Set an expectation that all children will be inclusive on the playground

When teacher and author Vivian Paley (1992) announced to her kindergarten class, "You can't say you can't play," she was announcing a new expectation of inclusion. When you say to children, "You don't have to be best friends with everyone, but you do need to be friendly to everyone," you're telling them that the expectation is that they will include anyone who wants to play.

You can then tell children that when they line up to shoot hoops on the playground, it's important that they include anyone who wants to join in. When they organize jump rope or Four Square, they need to make room for anyone who wants to play.

Once you've clarified your expectations, quick reminders before recess and a quick evaluation after recess can keep the goal of friendly inclusion paramount in everyone's mind.

Provide activities for children who are less interested in sports

Not all children want to engage in sports activities. It's important to provide activities for these children, especially if you observe them wandering around the playground aimlessly. Children who aren't engaged will amuse themselves, and not always in positive ways.

Inexpensive materials can provide opportunities for engagement. I suggest Hula-hoops, jump ropes, or chalk for drawing on the pavement. You can also create spots for simple games of Four Square or Hopscotch. Some teachers arrange a "walking club" where children walk the perimeter of the playground, counting their laps and improving their personal best.

Provide noncompetitive games

More game options can bring peace and cooperation to the playground. Classic, noncompetitive children's games such as Red Light Green Light and Fish Gobbler can provide a fun experience for everyone. There are scores of tag games such as Freeze Tag, Blob Tag (where every time someone is tagged they become part of the Blob), and my students' favorite, Toilet Tag (where the person tagged becomes a toilet until he's freed by being "flushed").

Before introducing new games, take the time to teach procedures for safe and cooperative play. One such procedure is "tagger's choice," where the person who does the tagging gets to decide whether or not she actually tagged a person. Especially at first, it's important that an adult supervise the noncompetitive games to make sure that they are safe, fair, and inclusive. It's even better if the adult actually plays with the children, setting a tone of fun and fairness.

There are a number of options for teaching and supervising these games. I have taken students outside for a five- to ten-minute mid-morning break during which I teach a group game. I then provide a simple direction sheet to recess supervisors to keep them in the know. PE teachers can also teach children age-appropriate, noncompetitive games. And you can divide game supervision among colleagues who supervise recess.

In Appendix B, you'll find resources for noncompetitive games.

Provide structures at lunch that promote a positive, friendly atmosphere

The lunchroom can be a place where cliques flourish, leading directly to bullying behaviors. It can also be a place where children have the opportunity to get to know everyone, leading to friendly inclusion.

Change lunch partners—every day

Early in the year, you can provide structures that will help students sit with a variety of lunch partners.

During the first week of school, fourth grade teacher Mrs. Ryan explains, "In this class we're becoming a community. Part of becoming a community is getting to know everyone. As one way of doing that, you're going to sit with a variety of lunch partners."

She reaches into a cup filled with students' names. "Shamika, you may pick a lunch partner," she says. "Whomever Shamika picks will sit with Shamika at lunch today. Tomorrow, that person will have a chance to pick a different partner." Shamika invites Rachel to eat lunch with her. Mrs. Ryan continues to pick names until every child has a lunch partner. Mrs. Ryan has already taught students how to invite someone to lunch and she has modeled what a friendly acceptance would look and sound like.

Down the hall in Mr. Bissell's third grade, children are matched with a lunch partner through the luck of the draw. They pick a multiplication flash card and "find their match" by finding the person with either the factors or the product that matches their card. In Mrs. Ruffles' first grade, Mrs. Ruffles simply announces a different partnership each day. "Ricky, you will eat lunch with Marie today." Although children might be embarrassed to choose a partner of a different gender, they willingly sit with a partner that Mrs. Ruffles assigns.

Mrs. Ryan, the fourth grade teacher, arrives a few minutes early to meet the children after lunch. She sees smiling faces and hears happy laughter. She asks Mrs. Zunick, the lunchroom supervisor, how things went. "They got along well," Mrs. Zunick says and notes that even some of the kids who avoided each other the previous year in the lunchroom looked like they were fine. For the next few weeks, students will continue to choose lunch partners until everyone has had a chance to sit with many different classmates.

Teach conversation skills

If children are to get to know one another over lunch, they'll need to know how to talk with each other and what to talk about. Mrs. Ryan teaches children how to have a conversation with someone they don't yet know very well. She asks, "What might you talk about if you want to get to know someone?" Children suggest topics such as family members, favorite after-school activities, or favorite animals.

Even with good topics, children can easily fall into a pattern where each person talks but neither listens to the other. I suggest using Interactive Modeling to explicitly teach how to listen to a lunch partner and respond appropriately.

You might have already taught these skills as part of helping children learn how to work with partners and small groups (see Chapter Four). Even so, the reality is that children may learn a skill in one setting (such as the classroom) but have no idea how that skill applies to a new setting (such as the lunchroom). It's important for students to see the teacher model any new application of a skill and have a chance to practice it before they're expected to use it in a new situation.

Provide structure throughout the year, if needed

Changing lunch partners can go on for the first six weeks of school, for the entire year, or for any length of time in between. Some groups of children learn quickly how to be inclusive; other groups continually need structure to protect an atmosphere of kindness and inclusion.

Those quick observations that I described earlier in this chapter can serve you well in deciding how to use lunchroom structures. Notice how your students are doing with partners. How do they do when you loosen the structure a bit? Are they ready for more independence or do they need slightly tighter controls? The goal is to keep the lunchroom safe and friendly for everyone, to protect against an all-too-common negative atmosphere in which bullying can flourish.

Provide structures to increase safety on the school bus

The bus is a prime environment for bullying. Supervision is minimal, older and younger children are mixed together, and some children spend long periods of time on the bus. Bullying behaviors that begin on the school bus often continue surreptitiously throughout the school day. Even though we have minimal presence on the bus, we can still provide structures that have an impact on the peace and safety of students' bus rides.

Safe structures

The Peaceful School Bus program, used in many U.S. schools, treats each school bus as an individual community. School staff members lead bus-by-bus meetings to promote safe, kind, and inclusive behavior on each bus (Dillon, 2008). A whole-school approach to bus behavior such as this is optimal, but classroom teachers can have a positive impact by using a modified version of these bus meetings. Children can spend a few minutes at the end of the day with the other children in their class who share their bus. With teacher facilitation, they can draw pictures of safe ways to be on the bus, or write about the kind words they'll use on the bus.

Often bus drivers develop structures that promote bus safety, such as assigned seats. Our job, as classroom teachers, is to support the bus driver in implementing these structures. We can check in with children to make sure that they're using their assigned seats and that they're using other structures the bus driver has set up.

Big buddy/little buddy

In multiple studies, younger children report being bullied by older children and older children report doing the bullying (Olweus et al., 2007; Smith, Madsen, & Moody, 1999). One place that age groups are most likely to mix is on the school bus. The challenge for teachers is to replace the attitude of "I can show that I'm powerful by making a younger child uncomfortable" with "I can show that I'm powerful by being a leader and taking responsibility for younger children." An effective way to do this is to help older children learn to actively take care of younger children.

Mrs. O'Hare, a kindergarten teacher, teams up with the fifth-sixth grade teacher down the hall from her to create cross-age buddy pairings. In the first week of school, the older students meet their kindergarten buddies at the school bus and walk them to their classroom. During the year they work on both academic and nonacademic projects together. They do research on mammals, go on field trips, and create holiday gingerbread houses together. Younger and older children alike look forward to Friday afternoon "buddy time."

The big buddy/little buddy strategy can also work for individual students. When Ray, a student in my third grade classroom, began to bother Jamal, a first grader, on the school bus, the principal and I each discussed the situation with Ray's mother, Mrs. Snyder, who came up with a promising solution to try. "Jamal is in Miss Cooper's class and Miss Cooper was Ray's first grade teacher," said Mrs. Snyder. "Ray loves Miss Cooper. What would happen if Ray went to Miss Cooper's class to help out? He could practice being kind to Jamal in that setting."

Ray went to Miss Cooper's class once a week to help her students with their math. Ray was proud of his role and would start reminding me a day in advance, "Tomorrow I go to Miss Cooper's class." Miss Cooper made sure that Ray's contact with Jamal was indeed kind. Soon Ray was Jamal's special protector on the school bus. Ray discovered that he didn't need to be mean to feel powerful.

Notice that we didn't force Ray and Jamal together. Ray went to Miss Cooper's class to work with all of the first graders.

It's also critical to know that this strategy worked well because Ray wasn't actually bullying Jamal, although he was trying out "bugging" Jamal in a way that could have developed into bullying if it had continued unchecked. In addition, Miss Cooper supervised the boys carefully. When there's a potential bullying relationship between two children, forcing them together can be dangerous.

Collaborating With Colleagues Who Supervise Students Outside the Classroom

In every school there are many adults who supervise children outside the classroom. To be successful in preventing bullying behavior outside the classroom, you'll need to collaborate with these adults and support them in the hard work of keeping the lunchroom, the playground, the halls, and the school bus physically and emotionally safe.

Begin by telling them about strategies that you've taught children and listen when they tell you about strategies that they're using in the settings that they supervise. I recommend something as simple as saying to the lunchroom supervisor, "We assigned lunchroom seats today; here's the diagram of where each student will sit" or "We practiced hand games that children can play when they've finished eating their lunch. Could you let me know how the hand games went when I pick the children up?"

You can also check in with outside-the-classroom supervisors about how things are going in their setting. When you ask, "How did my class do today?" you're communicating collegiality and support.

It's also important to collaborate with these colleagues in efforts to stop mean behaviors. It was the end of the lunch period when Suzanne threw food at Michele and called her "Mickey Meat Loaf." Mrs. Murphy, the lunchroom supervisor, reported the incident to the girls' classroom teacher, Mr. Adair. He arranged for Suzanne to give up her Quiet Time that day to help the custodian with cleanup.

Later on Mr. Adair met with Suzanne. "Michele is part of our classroom community," he said. "I'll be watching to make sure that you treat Michele kindly when you're in our classroom. I'll also be checking in with Mrs. Murphy to make sure that you're treating Michele kindly in the lunchroom."

If Mr. Adair had taken the stance that discipline in the lunchroom was "not my job," the unresolved incident would have surely spilled over into the classroom. It would have most likely escalated into increasingly mean behavior. To solve the problem of bullying, we need to treat everything that happens to the students we teach as "our job."

Communicating With Parents About Outside-the-Classroom Behaviors

Parents are more likely to know about some of the bus, cafeteria, and playground mean behaviors than teachers are. Parents watch their child get on the school bus and see others move away from their child, leaving him isolated. They see their child get off the bus at the end of the day, in tears, explaining that older children have stolen her hat or her lunch or drawn with marker on her coat.

Parents sometimes assume that teachers aren't interested in what goes on in the cafeteria or on the school bus. They aren't sure whom to talk with about outside-the-classroom issues. If you let parents know that you care about events outside the classroom, they'll tell you about them.

For example, if you've discovered that the playground is the place in your school where your students feel least safe, you might communicate with parents about this area of the school. Begin by sharing specific information about steps you've taken to create a safe environment on the playground. Then ask for their help.

You might include a statement like this in your newsletter home:

> We're working to make the playground a safe place for all children. The teachers on our team are taking turns supervising a large group game every day so that all children will have a closely supervised place to go at recess. Children report that recess is 'more fun.' However, mean behavior can still happen out of our sight. Please help us by letting us know if your child reports to you that he or she feels unsafe at recess. We all want recess to be fun for everyone.

Once you've made this overture, it's important to listen and respond immediately when parents do report unsafe behavior. Making school safe for all is a team effort.

K e y   I d e a s

The majority of mean behavior happens in the often lightly supervised areas of the school, outside the classroom.

Teachers can play a key role in preventing bullying in "hot spots" such as playground, cafeteria, halls, and school bus.

Observe students outside the classroom, if only briefly. This can yield rich information.

Teach students that classroom rules "go with them" when they move around the building, and model safe and kind behavior outside the classroom.

Collaborate with grade-level peers and outside-the-classroom supervisors to keep the entire school safe and friendly for everyone.

Promoting positive relationships between older and younger students may help prevent bullying.

Providing structures that increase inclusiveness in outside-the-classroom areas can help prevent meanness and bullying.

Chapter Six

Sample Lessons for Teaching Children About Gateway and Bullying Behaviors

• • •

Second graders sit in a circle on the rug. Their bodies are still, their faces serious and intent as their teacher, Mr. Monardi, reads aloud from *Nobody Knew What To Do: A Story About Bullying* (McCain, 2001). The vivid illustrations make the story real for each child in the class.

"Sometimes kids pick on me," blurts out Maya, a child with an autism spectrum disorder diagnosis. "I'd like to talk with you about that after the lesson is over," Mr. Monardi replies to her.

Mr. Monardi is pleased to see that Saul, Nico, and Frankie look deeply engaged with the story. Just last week he had discovered these three boys in the hall teasing Len about his lisp.

Immediately after the incident, all three boys lost the privilege of walking in the hall without an adult escort. Mr. Monardi knows, however, that to put a stop to future mean behaviors, he'll need to establish a class understanding about just how unacceptable such mean teasing is. The read-aloud is a good place to start.

In teaching this and other lessons about bullying behaviors, Mr. Monardi is establishing a vocabulary with the class. He is naming mean behaviors and establishing a common expectation that they are not acceptable.

It's important to teach children directly about bullying as part of prevention efforts. Through this direct teaching, we can reinforce the idea that cruel behavior of any kind—whether physical or relational—is unacceptable. We can also teach students what to do when they see bullying behavior—or for that matter, any kind of meanness—occur.

Notice that I put the focus here on the witnesses rather than on the person targeted. It's common to think that the solution to bullying is in the hands of the child who is targeted. This is not true. Although the child targeted for bullying behavior may sometimes be able to speak up for himself or leave the situation, this is often not a realistic—or safe—option.

Bullying behavior often loses its power without an audience to support it. Classmates can learn to befriend, or at least be friendly to, the person being targeted. Classmates can also learn to report cruel behavior to adults. Once a sympathetic adult knows about the bullying, the adult can protect the targeted child.

In this chapter, you'll find lesson plans for primary and upper elementary students that are designed to help children identify bullying behaviors, learn ways they can help the child who is targeted, and learn how and when to report bullying and pre-bullying mean behaviors. These lessons have been used in classrooms and are developmentally appropriate and engaging.

What Is in the Lessons?

Each of the five lessons takes between twenty and thirty minutes to teach. Each lesson has a version for primary grades (K–2) and one for upper elementary grades (3–5). If you teach third grade, I suggest you read through the lessons at both levels and decide which will best fit the needs of the students in your class.

Lessons for kindergarten through second grade

Bullying and behaviors that are gateways to bullying can begin in kindergarten and before. It's important that right away, as children begin school, we make clear that school is to be a place where they can feel safe and be safe. The first two lessons focus on helping children identify what is safe and unsafe behavior. I don't use the term "bullying" until the end of Lesson Two. This term might be a bit abstract for young children, who are still quite literal minded. They can, however, relate easily to such descriptive terms as "safe" or "included" or "kind words." Conversely, they can understand such concepts as being "teased in an unfriendly way" or being "left out." Of course, they know what it means to get hurt.

Once these basics are established, I introduce the concept of bullying at the end of Lesson Two and then the third, fourth, and fifth lessons address the issue of "bullying" directly, using that word. These lessons focus on the role of classmates in preventing bullying by letting adults know about unkind behaviors and by befriending or being friendly to the child who is targeted. These are both research-supported practices in bullying prevention (Davis & Nixon, 2010; Olweus & Limber, 2010). Since the majority of bullying takes place outside the classroom, there is a lesson about what to do if children experience bullying in such "hot spots" as the cafeteria or the playground.

> ### Use of the Word "Report"
>
> Throughout the lessons I use the word "report" rather than "tell an adult"—I do this because I want to avoid the negative associations that many children and adults have with "tattling" and "telling." I'm not suggesting that children need to "report" in an official way.
>
> In addition, the definition of bullying I use in these lessons does not necessarily describe behavior that is a reportable offense in your state. To understand when and how to officially report bullying, you will need to become familiar with your state's guidelines.

Lessons for third through fifth grade

The lessons for older children begin by defining bullying. The class then sorts scenarios to identify whether or not the situations are bullying. This activity will help students identify whether or not behavior that they see in real life is acceptable. They also learn some basic strategies for preventing bullying, which will help them know what to do when they observe or find themselves participating in real-life mean behaviors.

As children reach the ages of nine, ten, and eleven, they begin to define themselves by who their friends are. Children sometimes are reluctant to support a child who is targeted for mean behavior because they're afraid that then they'll have to be the person's close friend. For this reason, I have drawn a clear distinction between being friendly and being friends. It's important that everyone in the classroom be friendly and community-minded. However, just because a child is friendly to someone and supports her when she's teased or excluded doesn't mean that they need to be best friends.

Older children, left to themselves, are often reluctant to let an adult know about bullying. Many bullying prevention programs, however, have shown success in encouraging third graders to report to an adult. International research has shown that even fourth and fifth graders can feel comfortable reporting if the adults handle the information with sensitivity, allowing the child who is targeted maximum privacy (Olweus & Limber, 2010).

Structure of the lessons

At both levels, each lesson begins with information to help you plan and teach the lesson. I give lesson objectives, key phrases and concepts to keep in mind, and a list of any materials you'll need. Each lesson also includes follow-up activities designed to build student investment in creating a kind and respectful classroom and school climate.

Teaching the Lessons

Scheduling

These lessons will be effective only if you've begun to build a kind and empathetic community in the classroom. All of the strategies that

I discussed in previous chapters will set the tone so that children will be ready to receive the information that you'll teach.

In my own classrooms I taught bullying prevention lessons in October, November, and December. By mid-October the classroom community was strong enough so that children wanted to learn how to keep our community safe and friendly. Yet it was early enough in the year so that children could learn skills that they would then use all year long.

You may find that you want to repeat the lessons in the spring or simply do more of the follow-up activities in the early spring.

I recommend scheduling one lesson a week for five weeks. If you teach the lessons once a week, you'll have time to do some of the follow-up activities in between. If you let more time elapse between the lessons, you may find that the continuity is broken.

Developmental considerations

At the beginning of the set of lessons for each grade range, you'll find a list of developmental characteristics for the span of ages that you might have in your classroom if you teach within this grade range. I focus on characteristics that might affect how children respond to the content of the lessons or structures and give suggestions for how to use this information in your planning.

As you think about the developmental information, keep in mind the following:

- **All children go through developmental stages as they grow up.** Just as children's physical characteristics change, so do their social-emotional and cognitive characteristics.

- **Children go through the stages at different rates.** Although children in any given culture share some general characteristics at each stage of development, how quickly a child proceeds through the stages depends on many things, including the child's personality and environment. Some children achieve developmental milestones earlier than others. In addition, each child might mature more quickly in one area, such as physical development, but more slowly in another area, such as language skills. The developmental characteristics I list in the lessons are ones that have been commonly observed in students in U.S. schools. You may see variations among your students.

- **Children don't change suddenly on their birthdays.** For example, a child who just turned six might still display a lot of five-year-old behavior. By the same token, a child who is eight might display some nine-year-old traits.

For more information about child development, see *Yardsticks: Children in the Classroom Ages 4–14* by Chip Wood, 2007, www.responsiveclassroom.org.

Use of picture books

Many of the lessons are based on picture books. I've found that children can easily relate to the concepts at this slight remove. "What might DJ do next?" is an easier step than "What might you do in such a situation?" After you've taught and practiced what the book character might do, students may feel safe moving on to what *they* might do.

As part of preparing each lesson, I suggest you read each picture book all the way through for yourself. In the lessons, I give ideas for good places to stop and discuss, along with suggested discussion questions. You might go through the book and put small sticky notes on the pages where you plan to stop and discuss. When I used these lessons in classrooms, I often wrote the question that I planned to ask on the sticky note, thus preserving the flow of the lesson.

As with most literature-based lessons, students will doubtless benefit from many rereadings and discussions of these books. You may wish to begin by reading the book through with the students just for enjoyment. Many of the books have discussion questions listed in the back that you could use when you reread the book on another day. Some of the authors have websites with suggested classroom activities. You also can do these lessons early in the year and repeat them later on as a reminder and to take advantage of your students' increased maturity. The possibilities are endless.

In Appendix A, you'll find an annotated list of children's books that are especially useful for helping children talk about bullying.

The importance of classroom rules

The lessons are predicated on your having established classroom rules that students believe in and care about. When students have rules that they believe in, either because they created them collaboratively or because they have reflected deeply on how the rules will help make school a safe and fun learning environment for everyone, they have a shared vision of how school should be. This vision is the necessary foundation for learning to prevent and respond to bullying.

If you do not yet have rules that students care about, I suggest that before using these lessons, you spend some time creating rules that embody a shared positive community vision. Then you will have a basis for teaching specific positive behaviors that can prevent bullying. For more information about creating such rules, see Chapter Three.

Keeping things calm and respectful

Bullying and its prevention is a hot-button topic. It's stressful to talk about hurting and being hurt. However, we all, adults and children, think most deeply and clearly when we're calm and feel that our ideas are heard and respected. Furthermore, students mirror adults' emotions and actions.

For these reasons, it's important to lead discussions about such a potentially emotionally fraught topic in a calm, matter-of-fact manner that communicates respect. A calm tone will help students look at the topic thoughtfully. A respectful tone will help them feel comfortable sharing their true thoughts and feelings.

Model respectful listening

When you model respectful listening, children will follow your lead and listen respectfully to each other. Specifically, it's important to look right at children who are speaking, maintain a calm and nonjudgmental expression on your face, and acknowledge all of their ideas.

Expect children to treat each other with respect

It's important to expect children to treat each other with seriousness and respect when addressing this very important topic. Use immediate reminders or simple logical consequences such as time away from the group if students start to joke about what a classmate says or to use disrespectful words or tone.

Partner chats and group work

For these lessons to be effective, it is vitally important that the children are engaged. This is most likely to happen if they have plenty of chances to talk, rather than only sitting quietly and listening. For this reason, I recommend using lots of partner chats and small-group work.

Even kindergartners can turn and talk with a partner about such topics as "How do you think Ray is feeling?" or "What could you do to be kind to Chrysanthemum?" Because children this age may not yet be capable of then sharing with the class what their partner said, many experienced kindergarten teachers circulate, listening to children's ideas and then sharing them with the class: "I heard Juan say that he thinks Ray is scared" or "I heard Julia say that she would ask Chrysanthemum to play."

Children in first grade and up can usually turn and talk with a partner and then share with the whole group what they heard the partner say. With first and second graders, I suggest that you ask the whole group a question, have children turn and talk to an assigned partner (so as to head off any exclusionary behaviors), and then have children share out to the whole group.

For students in grades three, four, and five, you may want to pass out scenarios to partners or small groups, listen in while they work independently, and then have each partnership or small group share out. As they share out, you can lead a discussion about each scenario.

Investigating: Where do children feel safe and unsafe in school?

To teach Lesson Five about "hot spots" in school, you'll need to do some investigating. Most bullying prevention programs use some form of computerized questionnaire to learn about children's experiences with bullying. These questionnaires are designed for children in grade three and up. Many are based on the Olweus Bullying Questionnaire, which has been in use in one form or another for more than twenty-five years. Various other questionnaires can be obtained at no cost on the Internet.

You can also design your own questionnaire based on what you hope to learn and set it up on a free or low-cost Internet site such as Survey Monkey.

Here are some sample questions that you might ask:

- During this school year, has anyone kicked you, hit you, or pushed you on purpose in order to hurt you?

- During this school year, has anyone spread rumors about you to try to hurt your feelings?

> ### Social Media Use
>
> In the upper elementary lessons I refer to students using social media. Before talking with students about social media use, become familiar with your school and/or district's policies on student use of the Internet and social media.

- During this school year, has anyone spread rumors about you by texting, sending an email, posting on a social networking page, or using another electronic device?

- During this school year, has anyone called you hurtful names or teased you when you didn't want them to?

■ During this school year, if you have seen mean or bullying behavior happen (such as the behaviors described above) check off all the places you have seen it happen:

Walking to and from school; at breakfast; in the before-school program; in your classroom, the hall, or the bathrooms; during lunch, recess, PE, music or art; on a computer or cell phone; on the school bus; during the after-school program.

To determine frequency, you could ask children if the behaviors that they reported have happened: never, once or twice, at least once a month, or more than once a month.

A word about timing of the questionnaire

It's common to administer a questionnaire such as this one a couple of months into the school year so that children will be able to remember what has happened since school started. With end-of-the year questionnaires, children might have difficulty sorting out what has happened recently and what happened a long time ago.

Younger children

Bullying prevention programs don't usually use such computerized questionnaires for children younger than third grade. As an alternative, some programs use individual interviews for these children. Another approach is to create a large map of the school. Children place large dots on areas where they feel unsafe.

I suggest using a morning message that includes tally boxes (see primary grade Lesson Five for an example). You can ask, "Where do you feel unsafe in school?" and include boxes labeled "recess, school bus, school bathrooms, hall, cafeteria." Children put a tally mark in every box naming a place where they feel unsafe. Using this method, you can obtain data that will spark lively discussion about how to make those areas safer.

Specific Strategies Used in the Lessons

These lessons incorporate three strategies that will help children think more deeply about the difficult topic of mean behavior and bullying: role-play, open-ended questions, and card sorting.

Role-play

Role-play is a strategy for helping children think through a range of responses to potentially tricky situations. The teacher describes a situation that might present challenges and asks children to brainstorm positive ways to behave in the situation. The teacher and students act out some of the suggestions while the other students observe and comment on what they noticed. Role-play is used in the primary grade lessons in Lesson Four, when children think about how to befriend someone who is being targeted. Role-play is used in the upper elementary lessons in Lesson Three, when children think about how to be an ally.

I give a detailed description of role-play in Chapter Four.

Open-ended questions

Children are more likely to become invested in preventing bullying if their own thoughts and feelings are expressed, listened to, and respected. To help children express their thoughts and feelings, it's important to ask open-ended questions—questions for which there are many possible, acceptable answers. These questions encourage children to think deeply.

To help children believe that we do care about their ideas, it's important to then accept all answers that are even partially connected to the question. For example, when we ask, "How do you think Velvet felt?" children might answer, "Sad" or "Lonely" or "Happy that she had such a pretty name." Any of these answers are perfectly acceptable. If a child answers in a way that seems off base to you, you might encourage the child with such follow-up questions as "Tell us more" or "What makes you think that?"

For more information about open-ended questions, see *The Power of Our Words: Teacher Language That Helps Children Learn* by Paula Denton, EdD, 2007, www.responsiveclassroom.org.

It's also important to let children know when you're asking a question that has one right answer, which might happen with some of the more clear-cut sort card scenarios, and to think about how you'll respond if a child gives the wrong answer. For example, if you ask, "Is it bullying or not bullying for an older kid to tease a kindergartner in a mean way on the school bus?" you might alert children that this is a "one-right-answer" question by saying, "We've learned enough about bullying so we can figure out that there's one correct answer to this question." If a child responds, "When the kindergartner is teased by the older kid he must have deserved it," it's important to respond in a matter-of-fact way. In a friendly, calm, respectful way, you might say, "It's the job of older kids to take care of younger kids. Mean teasing of younger kids is nearly always bullying."

Card sorting

Several of the lessons are based on having children sort scenarios into categories such as bullying, not bullying, need more information. Whenever I teach these lessons on bullying I find that the discussions about "Is it bullying or not?" are rich and nuanced, with lots of gray areas. Those gray areas lead to deep thinking on the part of the group. I learn something every time I teach one of these lessons. With that said, I want to caution you to remain calm, not let unexpected comments fluster you, and honor all contributions while clarifying obvious misunderstandings. If you maintain an attitude of true curiosity, students will, too.

Facts to Keep in Mind as You Teach the Lessons

Following is a list of important facts about bullying and elementary-age children. All of this information is covered in depth in previous chapters of this book. I provide this list as a quick reference for you to review before you teach the lessons.

- Even very young children tease and exclude (Alsaker, n.d.; Pellegrini et al., 2007).

- If allowed to continue, these behaviors may become habitual (Wessler, 2003).

- Stopping the smaller mean behaviors can keep them from escalating into full-blown bullying (Wessler, 2003).

- All children have the potential to tease and exclude, even bully. For that reason it's important to focus on "bullying behaviors," not "the bully" (Swearer, Espelage, & Napolitano, 2009).

- Teachers are often unaware of bullying and hurtful gateway behaviors going on among students (Craig & Pepler, 1998).

- We will continue to be unaware unless we teach students to share this information with us. To stop bullying, we need to teach children to report (Davis, 2007a; Olweus & Limber, 2010).

- Increased supervision and increased use of consequences for bullying and gateway behaviors can significantly reduce bullying and support a climate of kindness (Davis, 2007a).

- Using the word "reporting" or "talking with the teacher" can encourage children to let adults know about mean behaviors. "Tell the teacher" has negative connotations for children and sounds like "tattling," which can also have negative connotations for children (Davis, 2007b).

- If adults respond effectively to children's reports, children will trust that we care about their safety and continue to report (Olweus & Limber, 2010).

- Children who are targeted for bullying behaviors are usually unable to protect themselves and need adult intervention (Pepler, Craig, & O'Connell, 2010).

- Telling children who are targeted to "ignore it," "stand up to the bully," or "fight back" is not helpful. These strategies have been shown to make the situation worse (Davis & Nixon, 2010).

- Doing assertiveness training for children targeted by bullying behavior or expecting them to talk out their differences with children who are bullying them is not helpful (Davis & Nixon, 2010).

- Bullying is a social act. When bystanders laugh, cheer, or even just watch, it encourages the behavior (Olweus et al., 2007; Craig & Pepler, 1998).

- Having at least one friend is protective against being targeted for bullying behavior (Hodges, Malone, & Perry, 1997).

- It can be risky for bystanders to step in and confront the person who is bullying. It's more realistic and safer for children to befriend the child targeted (Davis, 2007a).

- Most hurtful behaviors (gateway behaviors and outright bullying) take place outside the classroom (Astor, Meyer, & Pitner, 2001).

Primary Grade Lessons

■ ■ ■

Developmental Information

LESSON ONE:
Teasing in Unfriendly Ways Is Not OK

LESSON TWO:
It's Not OK to Leave Someone Out On Purpose

LESSON THREE:
It's Important to Let an Adult Know

LESSON FOUR:
Befriend Classmates Who Are Teased or Left Out

LESSON FIVE:
Hot Spots at School

(For upper elementary grade lessons, go to page 198.)

Developmental Information to Think About as You Plan and Deliver the Lessons

Five-year-olds typically:

■ **Are the center of their own universe** and seldom see things from another's viewpoint but can be surprisingly empathetic if someone is hurt (and they're not the one who caused the hurt)

Although kindergartners will most likely not become empathetic as a result of these lessons, they can still learn that it's not OK to tease.

■ **Respond well to "that's the rule"**

Therefore, as you read *The New Girl* in Lesson One, if kindergarten students don't make the connection that Shakeeta is feeling bad because she's being teased, move on and simply clarify that "it's the rule" that we don't tease.

■ **Need adult approval**

Five-year-olds are often eager to report mean behavior. If they take the information from Lesson Three and use it as a reason to over-report (and they probably will), be careful to encourage them in their reporting rather than shutting them down by saying "Don't tattle." (See Chapter Three for more information about the importance of moving away from the "no tattling" rule.)

■ **Have a hard time distinguishing between real and pretend**

With five-year-olds, it's sometimes helpful to use puppets when doing role-plays (thus making it clear to them that the situation you're acting out is pretend).

Six-year-olds typically:

■ **May be bossy, teasing, or critical of others**

When you read *The New Girl* in Lesson One, sixes might not think it's a problem for classmates to tease Shakeeta. It's important to be clear with six-year-olds that this kind of teasing is not OK.

■ **Take teacher direction seriously**

When you talk about excluding in Lesson Two, you'll need to state directly that excluding behavior is not OK.

■ **Often report hurtful incidents to the teacher**

Six-year-olds will take Lesson Three to heart. The teacher's challenge is to distinguish between serious and less serious incidents while erring on the side of taking children's reports seriously.

■ **Are eager to make new friends**

Six-year-olds will especially like the role-plays in Lesson Four, which focus on befriending a targeted child.

■ **Are active,** a characteristic which bursts out in lightly supervised areas of the school

The challenge for adults working with six-year-olds is to be very clear about which behaviors are mean as distinguished from behaviors that are simply rambunctious or impulsive.

Seven-year-olds typically:

■ **May find teasing to be particularly painful**

A good discussion focus for this age group is the difference between laughing with someone and laughing at someone.

■ **May find excluding to be particularly painful**

Yet this is an age when leaving others out is not uncommon. In Lesson Two, it's important to help seven-year-olds think about how the book characters (Velvet or Julisa) are feeling.

■ **Try out friendships and frequently change friends,** leading to lots of opportunities for hurt feelings

It may feel as though seven-year-olds are constantly complaining that a friend hurt their feelings. Nevertheless, it's important to take their reports seriously so that you don't discourage them from reporting.

■ **Often work and play best with one friend**

Lesson Four, in which children role-play how to befriend a targeted child, might feel challenging for sevens.

■ **Need clear rules and expectations**

Seven-year-olds are particularly helped when adults can work together to establish and maintain these expectations.

LESSON ONE:

Teasing in Unfriendly Ways Is Not OK

Grades K–2

Preparation

Objectives

Children will understand:

- It's important that everyone feel safe and be safe at school

- It's not OK to hurt someone's feelings on purpose (also referred to as "mean teasing")

Materials needed

- Choose one of the following children's books (see Appendix A for more information about the books):

  → *Chrysanthemum* by Kevin Henkes (grades K–2), Greenwillow Books, 2007

  → *The New Girl . . . and Me* by Jacqui Robbins (grades K–2), Atheneum/Richard Jackson Books, 2006

  → *William's Doll* by Charlotte Zolotow (grade 1), HarperCollins, 1972

■ Chart paper or other material to display simple drawing of a heart (heart icon) and simple line drawings of a flower (if you use *Chrysanthemum*)—fresh and wilted.

Key words and phrases

■ It's important for everyone to feel safe in school

■ To keep everyone feeling safe, it's not OK to hurt each other's feelings or bodies

■ Mean teasing (is not OK)

■ Safe and friendly

Procedure

Opening

1. Gather children in a circle. Have a flip chart set up next to you.

2. Begin by saying: *It's important for everyone to feel safe in school. To keep everyone feeling safe, it's not OK to hurt each other's feelings or bodies.*

3. Draw an image of a heart on the flip chart and say: *To keep everyone's hearts safe, we need to take care of each other's feelings and follow our classroom rule that says* _____ (choose a rule that conveys the idea of being kind or friendly).

Body

1. Introduce the read-aloud: *We're going to read a book that will help us think about taking care of each other's feelings.*

2. Read aloud from the picture book you've chosen, with the following suggested pauses and discussion questions:

The New Girl

➤ Read to the middle of page 6 (DJ calls Shakeeta "Shakeeta Mosquita").

Ask: *How do you think Shakeeta is feeling? Why might Shakeeta say "I'll punch you in the head"?*

Clarify that Shakeeta is probably scared.

➤ Read to the middle of page 10 (DJ tells Shakeeta she looks like an iguana).

Ask: *How do you think Shakeeta is feeling?*

➤ Read to the bottom of page 13 (Mia understands what helps Shakeeta feel at home).

Ask: *What might Mia do to take care of Shakeeta?*

➤ Read to the bottom of page 18 (when the girls laugh together).

Ask: *What is the difference between laughing at someone and laughing with someone?*

➤ Additional questions you might ask:

How might you feel if this were happening to you?

How do you think Mia feels when she's laughing with Shakeeta?

How do you think DJ feels when he tells Shakeeta that she looks like an iguana?

How might Shakeeta feel?

William's Doll

➤ Read to the bottom of page 12 (William's father offers him a baseball; his brother and a neighbor call him names).

Ask: *How do you think William is feeling?*

Chrysanthemum

→ Stop periodically (when everyone giggles at Chrysanthemum's name).

　　Ask: *How do you think Chrysanthemum is feeling?*

→ When Victoria says, "You're named after a flower," and Chrysanthemum wilts, explain the meaning of "wilt."

→ Draw a picture of a fresh flower and a wilting one.

→ Whenever Chrysanthemum wilts, have the children wilt with their bodies: *Let's make our bodies wilt.*

Closing

1. Say: *Sometimes people hurt other people's feelings or hearts—* (point to heart icon) *with mean teasing, just the way _____ (DJ, Victoria, William's friends) hurt _____'s (Shakeeta's, Chrysanthemum's, William's) feelings. This is not OK here at our school.*

2. Connect to classroom or school rules:

Which of our class rules would let _____ (DJ, Victoria, William's friends) know that teasing _____ (Shakeeta, Chrysanthemum, William) is not OK?

For first and second graders:

If _____ (DJ, William's friends, Victoria) were in our class, which rule would you remind them of?

3. Following are additional questions to ask, as appropriate:

Our school rule says _____. How does this help us know not to hurt others?

What can we do to keep our classroom safe and friendly?

How can we use friendly words?

What can you do on the playground (in the cafeteria, in our classroom) to make sure that everyone feels safe in school?

Take some ideas and then say:

The next time we meet we'll talk about some things that people have done to keep our classroom safe and friendly.

Follow-up activities

- Follow up frequently during the day: **How are you helping people feel safe in school?** Do this especially before the children leave the classroom for areas that require more independence, such as the cafeteria or the playground.

- Partner chat, morning message, or question of the day: **How have you seen people keeping our school safe and friendly? On the playground? On the school bus? In the cafeteria?**

- Plan greetings in which children practice the language of inclusion: "Good morning, [classmate's name]; I'm glad you're my friend" or "Hello, [classmate's name]; I'm glad you're here today." These greetings are especially effective when children are sitting in random order rather than with a "best friend."

- Sing a song that celebrates inclusion, such as "All My Friends Are Here Today," "The More We Get Together," or "We're All Back Together Again."

- For second graders: Learn and practice how to give compliments.

Additional children's literature to read

For all ages: Read or reread the picture books in the lesson.

Especially for first and second grade:

The Meanest Thing to Say by Bill Cosby (from the Little Bill series): When a couple of classmates introduce a game that rewards mean behavior, Little Bill's dad teaches him a strategy for staying true to himself and not being mean.

It's Not OK to Leave Someone Out On Purpose

Grades K–2

Preparation

Objectives

Children will understand:

- It's important that everyone be safe at school
- It's not OK to leave someone out on purpose

Materials needed

- Choose one of the following children's books (see Appendix A for more information about the books):

  → *Odd Velvet* by Mary Whitcomb (grades K–2), Chronicle Books, 1998

  → *Two of a Kind* by Jacqui Robbins (grades K–2), Atheneum Books for Young Readers, 2009

- Chart paper with icons drawn under the heading "Safe"

  → Heart icon from Lesson One

  → Stick figures holding hands icon (for including people)

- ➤ Puffy oval figure icon (for keeping people's bodies safe)

■ Examples of kind behaviors that you've seen since the last lesson.

■ Some possible examples of exclusion (for example, you can't go to my birthday party, you can't be in our club, you can't play the game with us, you can't sit here, I'm saving the seat for [classmate's name], you can't be my friend) either written or prepared to share orally

Key words and phrases

■ Important to be safe in school

■ Keep the classroom safe and friendly

■ Help everyone feel welcome

■ Keep everyone's feelings safe

■ Left out on purpose

■ Hurting someone

■ Say kind things

■ Include everyone

Procedure

Opening

1. Gather children in a circle. Have a flip chart set up next to you—have the icons visible.

2. Begin by saying: *(Last week/A few days ago/Yesterday) we talked about the fact that it's important that everyone be safe in school— we need to keep everyone's feelings as well as their bodies safe.*

3. Help children focus on ways they've kept each other safe:

> *What have you noticed classmates doing since (last week/a few days ago/yesterday) to keep our classroom safe and friendly so that everyone will feel welcome?*

> *Did someone do something friendly for you or someone else?*

> *These are things I've noticed you doing to keep classmates feeling safe . . .*

4. Say: *Today we're going to learn more about how to keep each other safe and feeling welcome in school.*

Body

1. Read aloud from the picture book you've chosen, with the following suggested pauses and discussion questions:

Odd Velvet

➤ Read first few pages. Stop after the line "No one was silly enough to pick Velvet for a play partner."

> Clarify the meaning of "odd"—that children thought Velvet was different. Keep the tone sympathetic to Velvet. Say: *That's what some children thought, that she was different, and they didn't want to play with her.*

> Ask: *How do you think Velvet felt when no one picked her to play?*

Two of a Kind

➤ Read to the bottom of page 4 (Julisa and Anna sit under the slide together).

> Draw attention to the difference between "no one is invited up" and "anybody is invited."

→ Read page 5 (Melanie and Kayla make fun of Anna and Julisa).

Point out that Melanie is teasing the way the child in the story you read in Lesson One was teased.

Ask: *How is Julisa feeling?*

→ Read to the bottom of page 14 (Kayla and Melanie run off with Anna).

Ask: *How is Julisa feeling?*

→ Read to the bottom of page 18 (Julisa sits and stares at her book).

Ask: *How is Julisa feeling now?*

2. Say: *Sometimes children tell other children that they can't play. They leave them out on purpose.*

3. Give specific examples (either on cards or orally): *Sometimes people say, "You can't come to my birthday party" or "You can't be my friend."*

4. Say the following, depending on grade level.

For kindergarten: *How might you feel if kids left you out or told you that you couldn't play?*

People feel sad when they're left out.

For grades one and two: *Thumbs-up* (or whichever signal you usually use) *if you've ever seen someone left out.*

We're going to talk about how to make sure that doesn't happen.

5. Say: *It's not OK to leave someone out on purpose at school.*

6. Ask: *If (Velvet/Julisa) came to our classroom, what would you do? How would you include her?*

7. Finish the read-aloud. Then ask these summarizing questions:

Odd Velvet

Ask: *How did classmates include Velvet?*

Two of a Kind

Ask: **What did Julisa do to take care of Anna? What did Anna do to take care of Julisa?**

Closing

1. Return to class rules. Say: **Our rule says that we will (take care of classmates, be kind, etc). That means that we won't leave people out on purpose. Remember from our read-aloud (last week/a few days ago/yesterday) that we won't tease people on purpose either.**

2. Point to heart icon: **It's important to take care of people's hearts.** Point to inclusion icon: **It's important to include people.**

3. If students seem confused by "leave out on purpose," clarify:

> **If your parent says that you can have only one friend over and so you invite one person, you're not leaving anyone out on purpose. If you tell someone they can't play at recess, you're leaving them out on purpose.**

4. Be explicit that leaving out on purpose, mean teasing, and hurting someone's body on purpose are bullying and are not OK:

> **When kids leave other kids out on purpose, when they tease someone in a mean way or hurt their bodies on purpose (refer to body icon), we call that bullying.**

5. Ask: **What might we do to include everyone at recess? What can you do today at recess to include someone?**

Follow-up activities

- Partner chat, morning message, or question of the day: **How have you seen people including others? On the playground? On the school bus? In the cafeteria?**

- Children will need more practice in sorting out behaviors that are not OK.

  Use specific examples: *If you tell some kids that you're having a birthday party and they're not included, that is not kind.*

- Before children go out to recess, ask: *How will you make sure that everyone has someone to play with?*

- After recess, say: *Give yourself a score with your fingers (one to five). How did you do at including people today?*

Additional children's literature to read

Read or reread the picture books in the lesson.

Eggbert, the Slightly Cracked Egg by Tom Ross and Rex Barron: A story about accepting difference in oneself or others.

The Pebble, a Story about Belonging by Susan Milford: A story about acceptance and belonging—a boy finds a pebble and takes it home.

It's Important to Let an Adult Know

Grades K–2

Preparation

Objectives

Children will understand:

- When we see someone being hurt it's important to take care of them by letting an adult know

Children will learn:

- How to report
- Whom to report to

Materials needed

- *Nobody Knew What to Do* by Becky Rae McCain (grades K–2), Albert Whitman & Company, 2001 (see Appendix A for more information)
- Chart with icons from first two lessons
- For first and second graders:
  - ➤ Column headings for sorting (Report to keep everyone safe/ Let it go since everyone is safe)

➤ Cards with potential incidents described. For example:

Someone cuts in front of you in line.

Someone sharpens his pencil at quiet reading time.

Someone reads a comic book at math time.

Three children tell another child that he can't play unless he's the baby.

One student secretly pulls another student's hair on purpose.

A student uses markers when the teacher said to use a pencil.

Someone talks in the hallway, which is supposed to be silent.

A student pushes another student into a puddle and laughs.

Key words and phrases

- Hurting people

- What do you do if you see something unsafe going on?

- Whom might you report to if you see someone being hurt in their bodies or their feelings?

- To keep ourselves and our classmates safe, it's important to report times when you see someone hurt

- Report to keep people safe

- Let it go since everyone is safe

- We don't need to report everything that we see happening; we can let it go, if no one is being hurt

Procedure

Opening

1. Gather children in a circle. Have a flip chart set up next to you—have the icons visible.

2. Begin by saying: *The last time we were together we talked about how important it is that everyone be safe and feel safe in school. Our rules say we should (take care of each other, be kind, etc.). That means if we see something unsafe happening we need to take care of the person being hurt. Remember when we talked about Velvet being left out (point to wilted flower icon)? Remember when the children teased (Chrysanthemum/Shakeeta/William)?*

3. Ask: *Have you ever seen someone being hurt in their feelings or their body and not known what to do?*

4. Hold up the book. Say: *Let's look at the cover of this book. It's called* **Nobody Knew What to Do.** *This story will give you an idea of what to do if you see someone being hurt.*

Body

1. Read aloud *Nobody Knew What to Do.* When the text refers to "bullies" substitute, "The kids who bullied."

- Stop after pages 5 and 6 and discuss: *What might they do?*

- When Ray doesn't come to school, comment that he didn't feel safe in school.

- Read to the end of the story. Ask: *How did Ray's classmates help him? How might you help someone who's being hurt as Ray was?*

> *Teacher Tip* ───────────────
>
> Some children will think that they should help Ray by telling him how to stand up to the children who were bullying. This is a good time to make it clear that it's the class-mates' job and the adults' job to take care of Ray. It's appropriate to teach children to use the skill of assertion when they are learning to deal with conflicts among children of equal power. When dealing with bullying, however, it is neither realistic nor safe to expect them to assert themselves. ■

> *Teacher Tip* ───────────────
>
> Young children often hit, kick, or push impulsively. This is not bullying (although it's also, of course, not OK). Often young children need direct instruction and practice

in how to use words to express their needs, how to take turns, and other ways to take care of themselves without hurting someone. The boys in *Nobody Knew What to Do* were purposely (versus impulsively) hurting Ray. Thus the school responded by increasing supervision and contacting parents. ∎

2. Draw attention to the fact that the narrator reported and that the next day the classmates included Ray in their play. The teacher, the principal, and the parents all got involved and worked together to make sure that everyone was safe in school.

> ***Teacher Tip***
>
> It's helpful to use the word "reporting" or the phrase "talking with the teacher" in teaching children to let adults know about mean behaviors because the word "telling" has such negative connotations for children. It also sounds a bit like "tattling," which can also have negative connotations for children. See Chapter Three for more information. ∎

3. For kindergartners:

Remind students of Chrysanthemum, whose feelings were hurt (refer to heart icon) like the boy in today's story, whose body was hurt (refer to body icon).

Ask: ***Whom might you report to if you see someone being hurt in their bodies or their feelings?*** Gather some ideas.

Ask: ***What might you say?*** Model one possibility and then take ideas.

> ***Teacher Tip***
>
> If kindergartners seem confused, connect Ray's situation to incidents that they do know how to handle. ***What would you do if you saw someone fall down and get hurt? What would you do if you couldn't turn the faucet off?*** These are other situations where it's important to report to an adult. ∎

4. For first and second graders:

Say: ***To keep yourselves and your classmates safe, it's important to report times when you see someone being hurt. You don't need to tell the teacher everything that happens; sometimes you can let*** *it go, if you're sure no one is being hurt. And if you're ever not sure whether someone is being hurt, talk with the teacher and she can decide.*

Have cards describing incidents prepared and, as a class, sort them into categories (see Materials list for suggested topics): Report to keep people safe/Let it go since everyone is safe

For each incident, refer back to icons and ask: *Was his body safe? Feelings safe? Was he included?*

Closing

1. Return to class rules. Ask: *How does reporting if we see someone being hurt connect to our rules? Which class rule will help us with this?*

2. For first and second graders:

Say: *Today we sorted situations and talked about which ones are most important to report. If you're not sure, it's important to report since it's so important for everyone in our class to be safe.*

Teacher Tip

If children do report unkind behaviors to you, it's important that you make it clear to them that they need to continue to report to you if the behavior continues—children need to report every time; otherwise you won't know whether the problem is solved. ■

3. This is a pretty serious lesson. You might lighten things up with a song or finger play about inclusion—for example, Red Grammer's "Kindness" or "We're All in This Together."

Follow-up activities

■ Partner chat, morning message, or question of the day: *How are we doing at keeping each other safe?*

■ Continue card sort with more incidents. Children will need lots of practice with this. If students are experienced at working as partners or in small groups, you might have them work with a partner to sort incidents and then place the cards in Hula-hoops or a pocket chart.

■ During writers' workshop, have children do "quick writes" that describe incidents that might or might not be important to report. Let students know that you might use some of the scenarios in class, with no names attached. Also let them know that you'll check in with them if you want to use their scenario.

Screen the scenarios and choose a few to type up (without names or key identifying information). Sort these scenarios with your students. Doing this provides an opportunity to discuss real-life incidents at a safe remove.

■ If you have a book that you're reading as a class, you might refer to incidents in the book. *Is a character feeling safe? Is he included? Is his body safe?*

LESSON FOUR:

Befriend Classmates Who Are Teased or Left Out

Grades K–2

Preparation

Objectives

Children will understand:

- By being a friend, we can help classmates who are teased or left out

Children will learn:

- How to approach and include someone who is isolated

Materials needed

Chart stand, chart paper, and markers

Key words and phrases

- Take care of classmates who are being teased or left out
- Being friendly
- Feeling included

Teacher Tip: Doing a Role-Play With Primary Grades

In this lesson, children will do a role-play about inclusion, using the characters from *Chrysanthemum* (or *Odd Velvet* or *The New Girl*). Here are a few tips to help this go more smoothly:

- Assign roles rather than asking for volunteers.
- Take the lead yourself the first time you do the role-play. After that, think about assigning the role of the "inviter" to someone who needs practice with this skill, assuming that the child is willing.
- For kindergartners: Use puppets rather than actual human actors.
- For kindergartners: In step 2, have the children partner chat before gathering ideas. Get some initial ideas on the chart by saying, "Here are some things I heard people saying to their partners." ■

Procedure

Opening

1. Gather children in a circle. Have a flip chart set up next to you—have the icons from the earlier lessons visible.

2. Begin by saying: *Last time we met, we talked about ways to keep people safe in school. We talked about making sure that everyone is safe, in their bodies and their feelings, by reporting to a teacher. We talked about making sure that everyone is included. We can take care of classmates who are being teased or left out by including them and being friendly to them.* (Refer to the three icons as you talk.)

Body

1. Set up the role-play:

Remember when we read about Chrysanthemum (Velvet, Shakeeta)? I'm going to pretend that I'm one of Chrysanthemum's (Velvet's, Shakeeta's) classmates. I can see that Chrysanthemum (Velvet, Shakeeta) is so sad because kids are teasing her about her name (because she's different, because she's new in school).

> *I'd like to help her but I'm not sure how. What might I say to her to show her that I'd like to be friendly to her and include her?*

2. Take ideas from children and list them on the chart.

3. Assign roles and describe what you will do:

   > *Now I'm going to pretend that I'm one of Chrysanthemum's classmates. Max, would you like to pretend to be Chrysanthemum?*

   > *I'm going to pick one of our ideas. I think I'll pick going up to Chrysanthemum and asking her if she wants to play.*

4. Begin the role-play:

   You and your student partner stand in front of the circle of children.

   You say: *Ready, start* or *Lights, camera, action* to indicate the beginning of the role-play.

   You say: *Chrysanthemum, would you like to play?*

   The student responds: *I'd like that.*

   You say: *Cut.*

   You ask: *What did you notice about our play?*

5. Children contribute ideas. If children have a hard time coming up with ideas, prompt them with questions:

   > *What did I do?*

   > *What did my face look like?*

   > *What did my hands do?*

   > *Max, when I asked you to play, how did you feel?*

6. The class continues to act out various ideas from the chart, this time with students playing both roles.

Closing

Point to the chart with the list of ideas. Say: *Look at all of the ideas we have for ways to be friendly and include people.*

Follow-up activities

- Partner chat, morning message, or question of the day: *Have you offered to include someone?* or *How might you include someone on the playground? In the cafeteria?"*

- For further role-plays:

  What if you try to include someone and they don't want to play with you?

  What if you try to include someone and they want to play a game that's different from the one you want to play?

Additional children's literature to read

For first and second graders:

Bird Child by Nan Forler: A girl is bullied and "bird child" steps in. This book provides a helpful springboard to discuss intervening when someone is being mean.

The Brand New Kid by Katie Couric: Lazlo is new in school. Classmates tease and exclude him, but Ellie befriends him. This book is a helpful springboard to discussions of befriending the person targeted.

LESSON FIVE:

Hot Spots at School

Grades K–2

Preparation

Objectives

Children will learn how to report if students are hurting each other outside of the classroom

Materials needed

- Chart with student responses about "hot spots" in the school

- (Optional) Morning message that asks children where in school they feel safe and where they feel unsafe. Under the questions, include lines or boxes for school bus, cafeteria, playground, halls, bathrooms, and other areas that might be "hot spots" in your school.

Dear Friendly First Graders,

We are working together to make school safe for everyone. Put a check in the box if you do not feel safe in:

School bus	Cafeteria
Halls	Bathrooms
Playground	Someplace else

Your teacher

Key words and phrases

- Where do you feel welcome?

- Where do you feel unwelcome?

- Where do you feel safe?

- Where do you feel unsafe?

> **Teacher Tip: Information to Gather Before the Lesson** ——————
>
> Before the lesson, gather information from students about "hot spots" in the school. There are many ways to do this. You could:
>
> - Interview children individually.
>
> - Create a map of the school and have students put a blue sticker on places where they feel safe and a red sticker on places where they feel unsafe.
>
> - Create a graph or chart and have children fill in boxes showing where they feel most safe and least safe, with choices such as halls, bathrooms, school bus, cafeteria, playground
>
> It's also important to gather information about adults to whom children can safely report.
>
> - Before you teach this lesson, think about whom children should report to about outside-the-classroom behaviors. Who would handle reporting with sensitivity and tact? Speak privately with those people about how they might handle reports.
>
> - Think about the lines of communication in your school. If you are going to encourage children to report to someone other than yourself, think about what that person will do with that information. How will you find out about the incident?
>
> - Alternatively, decide to simply have the children report outside-the-classroom unsafe behaviors to you. ∎

Procedure

Opening

1. Gather children in a circle. Have a graphic indicating safe/unsafe areas set up next to you.

2. Begin by saying: *Let's look at our graph (map, chart) together. What do you notice? Where do students feel safe? Where do they feel unsafe?*

Body

1. Say: *If something is happening (on the playground, in the cafeteria, in the hall—depending on what children have shared) that makes you feel unsafe or unwelcome, what might you do?*

2. Prompt children's thinking by referring to previous reading: *Remember when we read **Nobody Knew What to Do?** What did they do?* (In the story the children report to their classroom teacher.)

3. Ask: *Whom else might you report to (on the playground, in the cafeteria or hall, depending on area discussed)?*

4. List the names of the people the children suggest around the borders of your graph or map so that children can see that the adults at school surround them and keep them safe.

Closing

1. Point to the graphic. Say: *Look at all of the adults who can keep you safe! Think about which adult you, personally, feel comfortable going to if something unsafe is happening.*

2. Say: *Hold out your fist. Put out your pointer finger and think about one adult you could go to.* Take note of any children who don't do this and check in with them later about whether there are any adults they feel comfortable reporting to. If not, encourage them to report to you.

Follow-up activities

- Children draw a picture of someone doing something kind for them on the playground (or on the school bus or in the cafeteria, bathroom, hall).

- Children draw a picture of themselves at lunch, at recess, or on the school bus and chat about how things are going in that setting.

- Check in after lunch and recess. Ask children to hold up fingers (one through five) showing how safe and welcome they each felt today in the cafeteria and at recess. Ask children to hold up fingers to show how well each did at welcoming others.

- Drama: Have children write stories about a time when someone was kind to them on the playground, in the cafeteria, on the school bus, or in the hall. Pick some of the stories for the class to act out in small groups.

Additional children's literature to read

Yoko by Rosemary Wells: When Yoko's classmates tease her because she has sushi for lunch, Mrs. Jenkins, her teacher, plans an international food festival. Only one student takes the challenge of tasting some of Yoko's sushi but this is enough for Yoko to feel supported.

Upper Elementary Lessons

■ ■ ■

Developmental Information

LESSON ONE:
What Is Bullying Behavior? (Part One)

LESSON TWO:
What Is Bullying Behavior? (Part Two)

LESSON THREE:
The Courage to Be an Ally

LESSON FOUR:
Deciding When and What to Report

LESSON FIVE:
Hot Spots at School

Developmental Information to Think About as You Plan and Deliver the Lessons

Eight-year-olds typically:

- **Love to take on big projects but sometimes overestimate their own capacity**

For these reasons, eight-year-olds will often be very interested in the information presented in these lessons and may get excited about figuring out how to take care of everyone.

- **Are forming larger friendship groups and making new friends**

Eight-year-olds will be open to ideas about being more inclusive.

- **Have a growing sense of moral responsibility and are interested in fairness**

Lesson Three will be especially interesting to eight-year-olds.

- **May exaggerate**

Since the heart of Lessons Four and Five is building trust that if children report we will do something about it, it's important for us to listen carefully to the reports of eight-year-olds and take the reports seriously, in spite of their tendency to exaggerate.

Nine-year-olds typically:

■ **Like to work with partners of their own choosing,** especially same-gender partners (which can lead to gender-role-based teasing)

Discuss some of the examples from *Just Kidding* (in Lesson One) that are gender-role-based, such as Vince calling DJ a "Girlie." Nines need guidance to see that gender-role-based teasing is not OK.

■ **May begin to form cliques**

This tendency could lead to mean or exclusionary behaviors. Offer clear guidelines—you don't need to be best friends with everyone but you do need to be friendly and respectful to everyone.

■ **Are concerned about fairness**

Emphasize the fairness aspect of treating everyone respectfully.

■ **Are concerned about who's "in" and who's "out"**

We need to let them know that we will protect their privacy when they report.

Ten-year-olds typically:

■ **Work well with classmates**

Ten-year-olds will be open to thinking about how to avoid gender-role-based teasing.

■ **Are concerned with friendship and social interaction**

It's important, however, not to put anyone on the spot or lead any of the students to feel that the lessons are calling their friendships into question. Be sure to emphasize "friendly" rather than "best friends."

■ **Are highly sensitive to and able to resolve questions of fairness and justice**

Ten-year-old students will likely show lots of interest in these lessons and be concerned about how to make school safe for everyone. This is a good time for teaching expectations such as "be an ally."

Eleven-year-olds typically:

■ **Put lots of focus on cliques, who's "in" and who's "out"**

Carefully explain the importance of "being friendly" rather than "being friends" with everyone. Also be on the lookout for cliques.

■ **Feel that saving face is important**

It's important to use examples for the sort-card activity that are similar to what might happen in your classroom but not the same as what's going on in your classroom. Ten-year-olds need to be able to examine issues of bullying without losing face.

■ **Feel it's important to choose their friends on the basis of common interests**

It's therefore important to maintain a tone that says that it's important to keep everyone safe and behave respectfully to everyone, but that doesn't mean you need to be friends with everyone.

■ **Are less willing to let adults have a role in handling bullying problems**

Although they may be willing to report to adults, they will be more interested in student-centered solutions such as "befriend the person targeted."

What Is Bullying Behavior? (Part One)

Grades 3–5

Preparation

Objectives

- To engage children in conversations about the difference between bullying behaviors and nonbullying behaviors—conversations that will help them understand that bullying involves an imbalance of power and an intention to harm.

- To raise children's awareness of the fact that we often don't know another person's motivations: an act may appear to be purposeful and actually be accidental; something that seems accidental may be purposeful.

Materials needed

- *Just Kidding* by Trudy Ludwig, Tricycle Press, 2006 (see Appendix A for more information)

- Definition of bullying written on a chart:

  → Bullying is when someone is mean to someone else on purpose

  → Bullying might be using mean words or leaving someone out or poking and pinching someone

➥ Bullying might be to someone's face or it might be behind their back (for example, on a social networking site or by sending a text)

■ Chart with icons:

➥ Safe in:
Feelings (heart icon)
Being included (stick figures holding hands)
Body (puffy stick figure)

■ Cards with examples (bullying/not bullying) on them

Key words and phrases

■ You have a right to be safe in school: in your feelings, in your friendships, in your body

■ Keep yourself and your classmates safe

■ When someone is mean to someone else

■ When they are mean to show that they are stronger, more popular, or more important than the person targeted

■ Using mean words or leaving someone out on purpose or hitting, kicking, poking, or pinching someone

■ Which class rule might help keep people in this class safe from bullying?

■ How might we make sure that people in this class/school are included? Treated kindly?

Procedure

Opening

1. Gather children in a circle. Have a flip chart set up next to you.

2. Say: *You have the right to be safe in school. You have a right to be safe in your feelings, in your friendships, in your body. Which of our rules might help you be safe in this way?*

3. Introduce what you will do today: *Today we're going to read a book to learn more about how to keep yourself and your classmates safe, how to make sure that people in this class don't get bullied.*

4. Post definition of bullying:

- Bullying is when someone is mean to someone else on purpose

- Bullying might be using mean words or leaving someone out or poking and pinching someone (use icons to demonstrate that following class rules would entail taking care of someone's feelings, including someone, and taking care of their body)

- Bullying might be to someone's face or behind their back

5. Clarify that bullying doesn't need to be ongoing: *When people pick on others in this way, they often do it over and over, but you don't have to do it over and over for it to be bullying.*

6. For fifth graders, help them understand that bullying behaviors involve an imbalance of power between children by saying: *When someone bullies, they are being mean to show that they are stronger, more popular, or more important than the person they are targeting.*

Body

1. Introduce the read-aloud.

2. Read *Just Kidding,* pausing periodically to ask open-ended questions:

Read to page 2 (rock, paper, scissors).

> Ask: *What does DJ mean when he says "I am the joke"?*

> Make the point that when DJ says "I am the joke" he's saying that it just doesn't feel right to him.

Stop at page 3 (tree house), page 4 (playing field), and page 5 (on the school bus).

> Ask: *How is DJ feeling?*

> Ask: *What are some of the ways that Vince was mean to DJ on purpose?* (Telling him that you lose if he's on the team, calling him a girlie, telling him he's wearing PJs, poking him and pinching him)

Stop reading after the scene on the bus when Vince says, "I was just kidding."

> Ask: *How could you tell that DJ didn't like the teasing?*

3. Ask: *When is kidding fun? When is it mean?* Refer to the definition of bullying, "mean on purpose."

4. Use some examples to clarify "mean on purpose." Say: *How do we know when something is "mean"? It's tricky. Sometimes we wonder whether people are trying to be friendly or just being mean. Remember when DJ said, "I was the joke"? What clues did he have that Vince was being mean?*

5. Give an example of fun teasing: *Paul and Joey are good friends. They call one another by silly private nicknames and both smile or laugh about it. Do you think this is bullying or not bullying?* Ask the class to discuss and reach agreement.

6. Give an example of mean teasing: *Joey is new in school. The other students start calling him "Joey Baloney." They whisper this name to him when he's walking down the hall. Do you think this is bullying or not bullying?* Discuss with the class.

7. Introduce the sort-card activity: Children will look at an index card with a situation written on it and decide whether it fits in the category of bullying, not bullying, or needs more information. (Note: The situations that children will likely put in "needs more information" are mostly situations where intent is unclear. That's OK—in life we often don't know another person's intent.)

8. Begin as a whole group; then, with older children, you could continue the activity as partners or in small groups. If students do work as partners or in small groups, it's important that you have them share out at the end. Doing so will let all students hear a variety of examples and give you an opportunity to clarify any misunderstandings.

> *Teacher Tip* —————————————————————
>
> If fourth or fifth graders haven't had experience working as partners or in small groups, this is a time to first practice what partner work or group work would look like. How will you decide who will hold the card? How will you make sure that everyone gets to talk? What if you don't agree about whether or not your example is bullying? ∎

9. As an example of how to sort, refer back to the situations mentioned in steps 5 and 6.

Paul and Joey are good friends. They call each other by silly private nicknames and both smile or laugh about it. (Not bullying)

Joey is new in school. The other students start calling him "Joey Baloney." They whisper this name to him when he's walking down the hall. (Bullying)

10. Do the activity. The following scenarios are just examples—choose scenarios that will be relevant for students in your class. As children do the sorting as partners or in small groups and then share, probe. Ask: ***How do you know it's mean? What clues might you have if you were _____ (from each character's point of view)?***

> ∎ A student tells a friend he'd rather not hang out today—he has to do something with his family.

- Your parents tell you that you may have one friend over. You invite Sammy. Mo's feelings are hurt.

- You're going to have a birthday party. You hand out invitations in school to all but one person.

- A group of students are shooting baskets on the playground. They tell another student that she can't play with them.

- A student accidentally trips in the cafeteria and spills food all over another student.

- A student purposely sticks out his foot and trips another student.

- Mike and Saul are friends. Mike has chocolate chip cookies for dessert. Saul wishes he had one and snatches a cookie away from Mike.

- Elise says to May, "You have to give me your lunch every day." May is afraid that Elise won't be her friend if she doesn't hand over her lunch, so she does it.

Closing

1. Ask: *Which class rule might help keep people in this class safe from bullying?*

2. Say: *Bullying is against our school rules.*

3. Ask: *How might we make sure that people in this class/school are included? Treated kindly?*

Follow-up activities

- Finish reading *Just Kidding* later on in the day

- Either in a class discussion or other reflection format (journal writing, partner chats), ask: *When is teasing and joking fun? When is it mean and hurtful?*

- For a journal writing assignment:

  A time when I experienced bullying . . .

  A time I was left out . . .

  A time when someone teased me when I didn't want them to . . .

- Do a quick sort of a few more teacher-prepared examples (add them to the chart):

  → All the students in the class decide to make up silly nicknames. Together, they make up a nickname for everyone.

  → A group of students decides to make up silly nicknames. They call Sam "Sammy silly-face." Sam does not look happy about it.

Teacher Tip

Children (and teachers, too!) will need lots of practice and reflection to figure out which situations are and are not bullying. Teachers who have used these lessons have found that continuing to practice sorting and discussing possible scenarios has been helpful in figuring out when a particular behavior meets the definition of bullying. ■

LESSON TWO:

What Is Bullying Behavior? (Part Two)

Grades 3–5

Preparation

Objectives

- To teach children that using mean words, leaving someone out on purpose, or purposely kicking, hitting, or pinching are all bullying.

- To engage children in discussions about the difference between bullying and nonbullying behaviors.

- To help children understand that we don't always know another person's motivations. An act may appear to be purposeful and actually be accidental. Something that seems accidental may be purposeful.

- To tell children that bullying is not OK in this class or school.

Materials needed

- Choose one of the following books. As you choose, think about issues the students in your class will find meaningful (see Appendix A for more information):

  ➤ *My Secret Bully* by Trudy Ludwig, Tricycle Press, 2004: Katie bullies her close friend Monica and calls her names behind her back.

➝ *Trouble Talk* by Trudy Ludwig, Tricycle Press, 2006: Bailey says mean things, teases in public and humiliating ways, and spreads embarrassing rumors.

■ Definition of bullying written on a chart (from Lesson One):

➝ Bullying is when someone is mean to someone else on purpose

➝ Bullying might be using mean words or leaving someone out or poking and pinching someone

➝ Bullying might be to someone's face or it might be behind their back (for example, on a social networking site or by sending a text)

■ Chart with icons (from Lesson One):

➝ Safe in:
Feelings (heart icon)
Being included (stick figures holding hands)
Body (puffy stick figure)

■ Cards with examples (bullying/not bullying) on them

Key words and phrases

■ You have a right to be safe in school: in your feelings, in your friendships, in your body

■ Keep yourself and your classmates safe

■ When someone is mean to someone else

■ When they are mean to show that they are stronger, more popular, or more important than the person targeted

■ Using mean words or leaving someone out on purpose or hitting, kicking, poking, or pinching someone

- Which class rule might help keep people in this class safe from bullying?

- How might we make sure that people in this class/school are included? Treated kindly?

Procedure

Opening

1. Gather children in a circle. Have a flip chart set up next to you.

2. Say: *Yesterday (two days ago, last week, etc.) we talked about bullying.*

3. Refer back to the book you read in Lesson One. Review some ways that Vince bullied DJ.

4. Say: *Today we're going to learn more about bullying. Bullying might be to a person's face or it might be behind their back.*

Body

1. Introduce the read-aloud.

2. Read aloud from the picture book you've chosen.

My Secret Bully

Pause periodically to ask: *How is Monica feeling?*

Pause when you come to the part where Katie calls Monica "Mon-ick-a" and ask: *Does this remind you of Vince and DJ?*

Finish the story. Ask: *How was Katie mean? What did she do behind Monica's back?*

Trouble Talk

Pause periodically to ask: *How is Maya feeling?*

Stop after Bailey tells Brian that Hua likes him and Hua tells Bailey that she has a "big mouth."

Ask: *What does the phrase "No offense" mean?*
Is it OK to say something cruel if you follow it up with
"No offense"?
Have you ever had someone say "No offense" to you?
How did it feel? Did it feel safe?

Discuss the fact that asserting your feelings is not necessarily being mean. Ask: *When Hua tells Bailey that she has a "big mouth" is she being mean?*

Ask: *How was Bailey mean?*

Make sure that the children understand the following: When Bailey tells Keisha "No offense but your shirt is too small," this is overt mean behavior. When Bailey tells kids at school that Maya's parents are getting a divorce, she may not have overtly meant to hurt Maya—instead she thoughtlessly spread a juicy rumor.

3. Sort more scenarios (bullying/not bullying/more information needed). Choose scenarios that seem relevant to your students:

- Pete tells Mark a secret. Mark tells the secret to lots of other students at school.

- Kelly tells her classmates not to play with Addie at recess.

- Two students post pictures of a third student on a Facebook page without the third student's knowledge or permission. (*Be clear with students that this behavior is not OK even if it's not considered bullying—always ask someone's permission if you want to post their picture.*)

- A student posts pictures of his or her birthday party on a social networking site.

- James locks all of the bathroom stalls and crawls out underneath. Paul sees him do this and reports it, privately, to their teacher.

- Marty tells other students that Markeith was the one who locked all the bathroom stalls even though he knows it isn't true.

- Melissa, a fourth grader, tells Suzanne, a kindergartner, "You're just a little squirt and you can't sit here" on the school bus. (*Be clear with students that picking on younger children is not OK. It's OK to tell a younger child that someone else is going to sit there, but politely—not in a mean way.*)

- Lamar tells Jacob that he can't play with him today at recess but that he'll play with him tomorrow.

- Latisha likes to play basketball at recess. None of the other girls in her class play basketball. Marcy tells Latisha, "Only boys play basketball."

- Several students send a text to another student telling her that everyone hates her.

- A group of students sends a text saying unkind things about another student. (*Be clear with students that texts can be a source of mean behavior—kids don't see facial expressions or body language or hear innuendoes. When the text is forwarded to others who have even less information, the meanness can grow.*)

- Two students tell a third student, "We'll be your friend if you agree not to be friendly with [classmate's name]."

- Suzanne plans a surprise party for her friend Jenine.

- Jill acts as if she wants to be friends with Chrissy. Then she writes on Chrissy's new notebook.

- Maeve trips and spills some paint on Javonne's new shirt.

Closing

1. Let students know that they have a right to be safe in school: *You have a right to be safe in school. You have a right to feel safe in school. You have a right to be included in school.* (Use icons—safe in body, safe in feelings, and included).

2. Clarify that it's sometimes hard to tell when someone is being mean: *Sometimes it's hard to tell whether or not a person is being mean*

(refer to scenarios that provoked a lot of discussion during the scenario sort). *Whether it's on purpose or not, it's not OK to hurt someone at school. If we're accidentally hurtful to someone, we need to figure out how to fix it.*

3. Say: *The next time we meet we are going to focus on ways to help if you see someone being treated meanly or bullied. In the meantime, pay attention to the ways that people in this class follow our rules and help everyone feel included and safe in their feelings and their bodies.*

Follow-up activities

- For written or oral reflection:

  How do you know that someone is a true friend? What might you do to be a good friend?

  When have you noticed everyone being included? How do people in this class take care of each other?

- Practice inclusion with your students. Mix up seating so that sitting with a clique is not an option. Do activities that require students to work with many different classmates.

- If you read *Trouble Talk*:

  Finish *Trouble Talk* later in the day or on another day. This story has many rich examples that you may want to discuss at length. You may choose to read the story over a few sessions. One topic you may want to reflect on with students is "When is news yours to share and when is it private news?"

LESSON THREE:

The Courage to Be an Ally

Grades 3–5

Preparation

Objectives

- To help children begin to think about ways to move from being a person who joins in the bullying or acts as an encouraging bystander to being an ally or supporter of the person targeted

- To help children learn and practice strategies for becoming an ally through role-play

Materials needed

- *Say Something* by Peggy Moss (see Appendix A for more information)

- Chart paper and markers

- Chart with stick figures and labels:

    Person who bullies

    People who join in

    Bystanders

    Allies or those who support
    the person who is targeted

    Person targeted

- Cut-out paper figure

Key words and phrases

- Friends/friendly (the way you act toward someone)

- Person who joins in the bullying, bystander, ally, supporter

Procedure

Opening

1. Gather children in a circle. Have a flip chart set up next to you.

2. Say: *In school, it's important to be friendly to everyone. That doesn't mean that you have to be best friends with everyone, but you do need to be friendly and respectful. What does it mean to be friendly?* (If children have a hard time coming up with a list of friendly behaviors, prompt them to think of a time when someone was friendly to them.)

> For third and fourth grades:
> List what it means to be friendly.

> For fifth grade:
> Create a T chart and list on one side what it means to be friendly and on the other side what it means to be friends.

3. Read aloud *Say Something* by Peggy Moss.

> Ask: *What does the main character do that is friendly? Why does she sit with the girl who's alone on the bus?*

Body

1. Introduce the role-play you'll do today.

> Say: *We're going to do some plays about how a person might reach out to help a person who's being targeted for bullying.*

2. Set up the role-play (see Chapter Four for information about role-plays):

Pretend there's a person whom everyone teases, like the boy in the book. I'd like to help him but I'm not sure how. I want to make sure I'm safe and I also want to take care of him. What might I do?

3. Take student ideas for what a person might do and write the ideas on the chart paper. (Note: In fifth grade classes, students can do the charting. Set up two chart stands and have two students alternate charting the ideas—that way, one child won't get overwhelmed trying to keep up with writing things down.)

Teacher Tip

Have some ideas prepared if you think coming up with realistic ideas will be hard for students. For example:

Walk over to him at recess and say, "Would you like to shoot some baskets?"

Ask him, "Would you like to sit with us at lunch?"

Remind students about the way that the student in the book sat down next to the person who was alone on the school bus. ∎

Teacher Tip

When you choose a student to take the role of the person being excluded or left out, make sure that the child you choose is not someone who struggles with that issue in real life. Be sure to coach the child in how to respond positively. ∎

4. Choose an idea from the list: *I'm going to pick one of our ideas. I think I'll pick going up to the boy and asking him how he's doing.*

5. Indicate the beginning of the role-play by saying something like *Ready, start* or *Lights, camera, action!*

6. Begin the role-play: Turn to the "excluded boy" and act out the chosen idea: *Hi, how are you doing?*

   The boy responds: *Better now that someone's spoken to me.*

7. Stop the role-play (*Cut!*). Ask students what they noticed: *What did you notice about our play?*

8. Children respond with their observations.

9. Act out other ideas from the chart, this time with students playing both roles.

Closing

1. Share bullying chart. Let students know that in most bullying situations, several people are involved:

- Person who bullies

- Person who is targeted

- Bystanders: Can be a person who joins in, passive bystanders (who encourage bullying through their lack of action), or allies (like the main character in *Say Something*). Be explicit—the person who laughs at the bullying is being a person who joins in the bullying.

2. Use a cut-out figure.

> Say: **It's each person's choice which role they want to play.**

> Moving the figure around, ask: **Will you choose to help the person bullying? Will you be a passive bystander like the people in the story who didn't do anything? Will you have the courage to support the person who is being targeted?**

Follow-up activities:

- For reflection (writing prompt, morning message, etc.):

  When have you invited someone to sit with you or join a game that you're playing, or otherwise acted friendly to someone who was alone?

  When has someone invited you to sit with them or join their game, or otherwise included you?

Ask students to write in a journal:

If I saw (pick one of the situations from **Say Something***) what would I do? What might happen if I did that?*

A time when I was a person who joined in the bullying: I laughed at the person being targeted.

A time when I was a passive bystander: I watched but I didn't do something.

A time when I was an ally: I befriended the person being targeted or helped the person in some other way.

■ Make a connection to social studies: Learn about bystanders in history. Learn about people who had the courage to take a stand.

Additional children's literature to read

Reread *Just Kidding* and talk about how DJ stands up for the boy on the school bus.

LESSON FOUR:

Deciding When and What to Report

Grades 3–5

Preparation

Objectives

- To encourage children to report dangerous behaviors to responsible adults

- To distinguish between dangerous behaviors and those that students can handle themselves

> **Teacher Tip: Grade-Level Considerations for Grouping Children**
>
> In this lesson, children will consider scenarios and discuss which scenarios require reporting to an adult. Following are suggestions for how to group children for the discussion:
>
> Third grade—Teach the lesson to the whole group.
>
> Fourth grade—Divide the group into pairs and assign one scenario to each pair. Pairs then report out to the whole group.
>
> Fifth grade—Divide the class into groups of four. Small groups consider the scenarios and then report out to the whole class. ■

Materials needed

- Chart showing difference between situations students can resolve and situations they need to report

Situations you can resolve yourself or let go	Situations you need to report
"He cut in line."	Help keep someone safe; for example, people are telling a child he can't play at recess.

- Cards with situations on them (I include suggested situations below but you may want to write up your own scenarios based on events that have happened in your classroom)

- *Just Kidding* by Tracy Ludwig

- The following books to hold up and refer to if it's been some time since students have heard either story:

  My Secret Bully

  Trouble Talk

Key words and phrases

- Reporting the behavior to keep someone safe

- It's important to report if someone is being hurt (physically, with words, or with actions such as excluding)

- When you report, I will keep your information confidential

- All of us have the job of keeping everyone safe

Procedure

Opening

1. Read from *Just Kidding*, starting where it says, "I'd like to say that Vince stopped bugging me after that, but he didn't." Read the next two and a half pages.

2. Ask: ***In Just Kidding, when DJ tells his dad about the ways that Vince is treating him, what do he and his dad do?***

3. One of the strategies that they use is reporting the behavior to DJ's teacher. Ask: ***How does DJ's teacher help?*** (She talks to the guidance counselor about helping DJ make new friends. She also watches out to make sure that everyone's safe in the class.)

(In *My Secret Bully*, Monica reports to her mother. In *Trouble Talk*, Maya reports to the school counselor.)

4. Say: ***When you're younger, people sometimes say "don't tattle," and so young children sometimes get the idea that telling an adult when someone is being hurt is not a good idea. In this classroom, I want to know about any hurtful behavior. When you tell me about this kind of behavior, we'll call it reporting. Reporting is about letting responsible adults know when someone is being hurt, when someone is the target of mean behavior that they can't protect themselves from. Reporting can be about something that you see done to someone else or something that's happening to you. It's to help someone who is in trouble.***

Body

Consider scenarios and for each one talk about whether children should report to an adult or take care of the situation on their own. Acknowledge that some situations will fall in a gray area. Suggested scenarios:

- Molly gets on the school bus. Sarah, Becky, and Maeve all quickly rearrange their backpacks so that there's no room for Molly.

- You're about to sit down on the school bus next to your friend. Sam quickly sits down right where you were going to sit.

- You're in the bathroom. Someone in your grade does something mean to a younger child. He or she says to you, "Don't tell."

- Paul, a first grader, gets on the bus wearing a new hat. Finn and Gabe, who are in your grade, snatch Paul's hat, throwing it around the bus and laughing.

- It's writing time and Finn doesn't have a pencil. He takes Gabe's pencil.

- Allen has just begun a new school. In the halls and lunchroom, when the teacher isn't listening, kids have begun to call him "Fat Albert" and laugh in a mean way.

- Kate and Anna are friends. Anna is good at sports and schoolwork. Kate has difficulty learning. The kids call Kate "dumb" and tell Anna that they won't hang out with her unless she drops Kate.

- Paulina is hoping to spend time at recess with Beth. Beth tells her that she needs to have a private conversation with Lavonne today but she'll spend time with Paulina tomorrow.

- It's recess time and a group of students are playing Knock Out. Some other students gather around and start cheering for the players to get a specific player "out."

Closing

Say:

If you're unsure about whether or not to report something, report it. It's always better to err on the side of keeping everyone safe.

If you report and the problem persists, report again. The adults around you may believe that the problem is solved unless you let them know.

It's important to report if someone is being hurt (physically or emotionally, with words or with actions). When you report I will keep your information confidential to keep you safe.

Teacher Tip ──────────────────────────

To ensure confidentiality, communicate with other adults in school ahead of time to make sure that they understand the need for confidentiality. If in doubt, tell children to report only to you. ■

Follow-up activities

- Partner chat, group discussion, journal writing:

  Why are students reluctant to report?

  What's the worst thing that could happen if you report? The best thing that could happen?

  What can adults do to help make reporting safe?

- Journal writing:

  A time when I thought about reporting.

  A time when I did report.

- For older children, journal writing or a discussion:

  What could the adults in school do to make it feel safe to report? What do you hope that the adult does? Doesn't do?

  Is it easier to report about other students being left out or about being left out yourself?

Hot Spots at School

Grades 3–5

Note: Before doing this lesson, you'll need to have gathered data about where in the school children feel safest and least safe.

Preparation

Objectives

- To help students think about how to keep themselves and their classmates safe in the lunchroom and on the playground and school bus

- To use information gained through questionnaire (Where do you feel safe or unsafe in school?) to help children think specifically about keeping themselves and classmates safe in identified "hot spot" areas

Materials needed

Chart with results of questionnaire (numbers covered)

Key words and phrases

- Felt unsafe

- What might we do

- Make the [name of "hot spot"] safer for everyone

Procedure

Opening

1. Gather children in a circle. Have a flip chart with questionnaire data set up next to you.

2. Say: *Recently, you answered some questions about where you feel safe or unsafe in school.*

3. Ask: *Where do you imagine people felt unsafe? Cafeteria? Bathrooms? Halls? Playground?*

4. Students chat with a partner and then share out their ideas.

5. Reveal the data on the chart, sharing the number of students who felt unsafe in the places in school that stood out as the "hot spots."

Body

1. Ask: *What have you noticed in the [name of "hot spot"] that makes it feel unsafe? Why do you think those behaviors happen there?*

2. Go around the circle with students reporting what they've noticed or why they think these behaviors happen in the "hot spot." Remind students not to mention people's names.

3. Say: *We've learned that it helps when students report mean behaviors to an adult at school or an adult at home. It helps when other students include the student being targeted.*

4. Ask: *What might you do to make the [name of "hot spot"] safer and take care of each other?*

5. Go around the circle again, brainstorming. Say: *Remember, when we brainstorm, everyone's ideas count. We'll accept all ideas and leave out our comments for now.*

6. Record student ideas on a chart (for fifth graders, have two students record ideas).

Closing

1. Sort the listed ideas, using questions such as:

Might this idea be effective in making the [name of "hot spot"] safer for everyone?

Is this idea realistic? Would it make a difference?

Which idea might you feel safe/comfortable trying?

We know that reporting to adults helps. What might the adults do to help you feel safe reporting?

2. As a class, choose an idea or two to try.

Follow-up activities

- Upon their return from an identified "hot spot," ask children how the idea that they picked worked. Did it help make the area feel safer for everyone?

- If students report that the strategy that they picked isn't helping, revisit the issue and choose another strategy to try.

- For morning meeting, question of the day:

  What can you do today in the cafeteria to make sure that every-one has someone to sit with? At recess to make sure everyone has someone to play with?

  What would you do if you saw someone else being picked on? Left out?

Additional children's literature to read

Reread *Say Something*, with particular attention to cafeteria scenes.

The Challenge of Kindness

• • •

We serve as powerful models for students—they will behave as they see us behave. When we speak kindly to students and colleagues, students will be much more likely to speak kindly to each other. When we work collaboratively and equitably with colleagues, students will notice us and will be more willing to work collaboratively and equitably with classmates.

In this book I've described many strategies that you can use to create a culture of kindness in the classroom. These strategies include creating classroom rules that children believe in, teaching and reinforcing kind behaviors, and responding quickly and nonpunitively to mean behaviors. But we need to go further. To be effective in bullyproofing our classrooms, it's essential that we model, day in and day out, the kind and respectful behavior we want the children to embrace.

This is not always easy to do. Respectful work with our colleagues means speaking kindly and respectfully to them even when we disagree with them. Respectful work with students means speaking kindly and respectfully to them even when we're setting limits or responding to their mean behaviors. Respectful behaviors toward students' parents means listening carefully and trying to see things from their point of view, even when we're having a difficult conversation about a child's behavior (or even when we see things differently—or view a child's behavior differently). We educators need to be the change we want to see in the world.

The problem of bullying is actually the challenge of kindness. Our media surround children with a culture of meanness—this is what they learn, over and over, about how to behave and be successful in the world.

But you can change things. Using the strategies in this book, you can create a safe, kind, and joyful climate in your classroom and your school and model kind and respectful behavior in all your social interactions. You can create a climate where children gain social recognition for their courage and their kindness, rather than their cruelty and misuse of power. Only a climate of courage and kindness can truly solve the problem of bullying.

Children's Literature to Use in Bullying Prevention Work

· · ·

Reading fine children's literature together, whether a picture book or a chapter book, is an effective community builder whatever grade you teach. I can still remember the books that my fifth grade teacher read aloud to our class. Many of us had tears trickling down our faces during the last chapter of *A Tale of Two Cities*. Over more than thirty years of teaching, I read aloud to my students every day.

Books can help children envision an ideal of friendliness and caring. They can show children how they might handle a tricky ethical situation. They can become a powerful shared class experience to revisit and discuss.

Sharing and discussing a piece of literature can also be a safe way to begin a conversation about bullying. Sometimes starting off by addressing the issue directly can lead children, especially older children, to feel defensive. Some children may feel that the class is discussing mean behaviors because they themselves have done something bad, which could serve to close down discussion. In contrast, the indirect approach of discussing the actions of characters in books can open up the issue in a way that feels safe to everyone.

Because of the power of a shared literature experience, it's important to carefully select the books that you plan to read as part of your bullying prevention program.

Choose books that focus on children's interactions rather than an analysis of why children might bully. We know that many people have the potential to engage in bullying behavior. Children jockey for power in this way for all sorts of reasons. It really doesn't help the child who is a target or her classmates to read an analysis of why the child who is doing the bullying is engaging in that hurtful behavior.

Choose books that encourage children to report mean behavior. Avoid books that make fun of children who "tattle." We want to encourage children to report rather than filling their heads with fears of being like the child whose tongue grew right out of his mouth from too much tattling.

Choose books that paint a realistic picture of how to respond to a bullying situation, with an emphasis on children taking care of each other and adults responding effectively. Books where the child who bullies magically discovers that the target is actually "cool" build an unrealistic image of how to solve the problem of bullying. The very best books show children learning about and taking care of each other. They also show the adults at school responding sympathetically and effectively when they learn about bullying.

Being a Bystander

Bird Child **by Nan Forler, illustrated by François Thisdale**
Tundra Books 2009
Picture book, grades 1–5

Eliza's mother teaches her to "fly," to "look down and see what is, look up and see what can be." When a new girl is bullied at school, Eliza protects her and teaches her to fly.

The Brand New Kid **by Katie Couric, illustrated by Marjorie Priceman**
Doubleday 2000
Picture book, grades 1–5

Lazlo is new in school. The other students taunt him and exclude him. When Ellie plays with him after school, she discovers that he's fun to be with.

The Meanest Thing to Say **by Bill Cosby (from the Little Bill series),
illustrated by Varnette P. Honeywood**
Scholastic 1997
Picture book, grades K–2

When a couple of classmates introduce a game that rewards mean behavior, Little Bill's dad teaches him a strategy for staying true to himself and not being mean.

Say Something **by Peggy Moss, illustrated by Lea Lyon**
Tilbury House 2004
Picture book, grades 3–9

The book is set in a middle school where some children are pushed, teased, and excluded. The main character would never engage in those behaviors, but she remains silent. Then one day she is teased and wishes that those around her had said something. This book includes an after-word for students with additional information about bullying prevention.

Children Taking Care of Each Other

Alfie Gives a Hand, **written and illustrated by Shirley Hughes**
Red Fox 2007
Picture book, grades preK–K

Reluctant to go to the birthday party without his mom, Alfie brings his blanket along. Finally he puts down his blanket to take care of Min, who is crying.

Those Shoes **by Maribeth Boelts, illustrated by Noah Z. Jones**
Candlewick 2007
Picture book, grades K–5

Just about everyone at school has a certain pair of shoes, but Jeremy's grandmother can't afford to buy them for him. They find a pair at a thrift store, but they're really too small for Jeremy. He gives them to his friend who also longs for "those shoes." This book also builds empathy for children whose families have limited financial resources.

Excluding and Including

***My Secret Bully* by Trudy Ludwig, illustrated by Abigail Marble**
Tricycle Press 2005
Picture book, grades 2–6

Katie and Monica have been friends since kindergarten. Lately Katie has been excluding Monica and calling her names. Monica discusses the problem with her mom and realizes that it's not her fault. She tells Katie that "friends don't do that to friends," and finds other girls to spend her time with.

***The New Girl . . . and Me* by Jacqui Robbins, illustrated by Matt Phelan**
Atheneum/Richard Jackson Books 2006
Picture book, grades K–2

When a new girl joins the class, children exclude her—except for Mia, who decides to befriend her.

***Two of a Kind* by Jacqui Robbins, illustrated by Matt Phelan**
Atheneum Books for Young Readers 2009
Picture book, grades K–3

When Kayla and Melanie play together, they don't invite anyone else to join them. When Julisa and Anna play together, everyone's invited. Then Kayla and Melanie include Anna but exclude Julisa.

Respecting and Appreciating Differences

***Eggbert, the Slightly Cracked Egg* by Tom Ross, illustrated by Rex Barron**
Paperstar 1997
Picture book, grades K–3

Eggbert is sent away from the refrigerator because he has a crack. He travels the world looking for a home and discovers that being cracked isn't so bad. This is a story about accepting difference in oneself and others.

***Giraffes Can't Dance* by Giles Andrae, illustrated by Guy Parker-Rees**
Orchard 2001
Picture book, grades K–2

The animals tease Gerald the giraffe because he can't dance. Then Cricket helps Gerald find his song and he learns to dance. This is a great story for second grade readers' theater.

***The Junkyard Wonders*, written and illustrated by Patricia Polacco**
Philomel 2010
Picture book, grades 1–4

Based on her own experiences as a student with special needs, Polacco has written a book that builds appreciation of children who learn differently. Caution: This story mentions the death of a student.

***Odd Velvet* by Mary E. Whitcomb, illustrated by Tara Calahan King**
Chronicle Books 1998
Picture book, grades K–3

Velvet is different from the other children. Although the children are polite to her, they don't ask her to play. Then, with some help from the teacher, they discover Velvet's special qualities. This is a good one for issues arising from income differences.

***One Green Apple* by Eve Bunting, illustrated by Ted Lewin**
Clarion Books 2006
Picture book, grades 2–6

Farah is new in her school and in the United States. She doesn't speak English. Told from the point of view of an immigrant child, this story builds empathy for recently arrived immigrants.

***Pebble: A Story About Belonging*, written and illustrated by Susan Milford**
HarperCollins Children's Books 2007
Picture book, grades K–5

The pebble wanted a special role in the world; it "longed for more." A boy finds the pebble on the beach and takes it home. It says, "I have found what I was looking for."

***Thank you Mr. Falker*, written and illustrated by Patricia Polacco**
Philomel Books 1998
Picture book, grades 1–4

Mr. Falker sees the potential in a student and helps her learn. Based on Patricia Polacco's own experiences, this book builds empathy for students with special needs.

***The Ugly Duckling* by Hans Christian Andersen, adapted and illustrated by Jerry Pinkney**
Morrow Junior Books 1999
All ages

In this classic tale, an ugly duckling is teased by his siblings. He grows up to be not a duck at all but a graceful swan.

***Weslandia* by Paul Fleischman, illustrated by Kevin Hawkes**
Candelwick 2002
Picture book, grades 3–5

Wesley marches to his own drummer. He has "no friends but plenty of tormentors." Over the summer, he founds his own civilization in his backyard. His schoolmates are curious and slowly he allows them to join in. This is a book about getting to know and like yourself and the power of following your dreams.

***Wings*, written and illustrated by Christopher Meyers**
Scholastic Press 2000
Picture book, grades 3–6

Icarus Jackson has wings. Children tease him. With the help of a friend, he regains his sense of pride and allows himself to soar.

Someone Is Bullied

Blubber by Judy Blume
Yearling 1974
Chapter book, grades 4–6

Caroline and Wendy tease Linda about her weight. Jill joins in. During the course of the book, the tables turn, and Jill is targeted. She gains new understanding about her mean behavior toward Linda.

The Hundred Dresses by Eleanor Estes, illustrated by Louis Slobodkin
Harcourt, Inc. 1944
Chapter book, grades 3–6

Peggy enjoys "having fun with" Wanda, in other words, teasing her. Maddie goes along because she's afraid that if she doesn't, she might be targeted next. Despite the fact that this book was first published in 1944, its message still rings true.

Just Kidding by Trudy Ludwig, illustrated by Adam Gustavson
Tricycle Press 2006
Picture book, grades 3–6

DJ's schoolmate Vince makes fun of him, pokes him, and sticks chewed gum on his chair. Vince brushes it off by saying, "Just kidding." With support from his dad and his teacher, DJ makes new friends who "have fun— without making fun of each other." This book includes information for adults about bullying and discussion questions for you to use with your class.

Nobody Knew What to Do by Becky Ray McCain, illustrated by Todd Leonardo
Albert Whitman & Company 2001
Picture book, grades 1–3

A group of boys bully Ray, who's new in school. The main character reports to his teacher. The teacher, principal, and the children's parents help stop the bullying behavior. This book includes information for adults about bullying prevention.

Trouble Talk **by Trudy Ludwig, illustrated by Mikela Prevost**
Tricycle Press 2008
Picture book, grades 1–4

Bailey loves to spread rumors and say unkind things, prefaced by "no offense." When Bailey spreads an untrue rumor about Maya, Maya talks with the school psychologist about it. Mrs. Bloom says that she'll work with Bailey and talk with the whole class about sharing information that's not theirs to share. In the meantime, she tells Maya, "Spend time with people who make you feel safe." This book includes information for adults about bullying and discussion questions for you to use with your class.

Teasing

Chrysanthemum, **written and illustrated by Kevin Henkes**
Greenwillow Books 2007
Picture book, grades K–3

The children tease Chrysanthemum about her name. Mrs. Twinkle, whose first name is Delphinium, saves the day.

William's Doll **by Charlotte Zolotow, illustrated by**
William Pène Du Bois
HarperCollins 1972
Picture book, grades K–2

William wants a doll. His brother says he's "creepy." The boys next door call him a sissy. His father wants him to play with more "manly" toys. Finally, his grandmother buys him a doll and helps William's father understand why William has wished for one—so that he can grow up to be a good father. This is a good one for issues of gender conformity.

***Yoko*, written and illustrated by Rosemary Wells**
Hyperion Books 1998
Picture book, grades K–3

Yoko's classmates tease her because she has sushi for lunch. To increase the children's appreciation of different foods, Mrs. Jenkins, her teacher, plans an international food festival. Only one student takes the challenge of tasting some of Yoko's sushi but this is enough for Yoko to feel supported. This book is good for issues about nationality and the power of friendship.

Resources

• • •

Bullying and Bullying Prevention

Books

The Bully, the Bullied, and the Bystander: From Preschool to High School—How Parents and Teachers Can Help Break the Cycle of Violence by Barbara Coloroso, updated edition, William Morrow Paperbacks, 2009.

Barbara Coloroso is a consultant and lecturer on parenting, teaching, and positive school climate. This book, first published in 2003 and recently updated, is clear, thoughtful, and carefully researched. The scope is broad and for that reason the specific information about how to prevent bullying in school is limited to one chapter.

Confronting Bullying: Literacy as a Tool for Character Education by Roxanne Henkin, Heinemann, 2005.

Roxanne Henkin is a professor of literacy education at University of Texas and is director of the San Antonio Writing Project. In this book she describes how to use reader response and reflective writing to build children's awareness of the importance of a safe and inclusive climate for all—includes lesson plans and a detailed bibliography.

Dear Bully: Seventy Authors Tell Their Stories, edited by Carrie Jones and Megan Kelley Hall, Harper Teen, 2011.

Young adult authors tell about their own experiences with bullying. Some of their experiences are relevant to bullying in elementary school.

243

Empowering Bystanders in Bullying Prevention: Grades K–8 by Stan Davis, with Julia Davis, Research Press, 2007.

Stan Davis has many years' experience as a school guidance counselor and consultant to schools on bullying prevention. This book offers research-based, practical strategies that student bystanders can use in response to bullying.

The Respectful School: How Educators and Students Can Conquer Hate and Harassment by Stephen Wessler, with contributions by William Preble, Association for Supervision and Curriculum Development, 2003.

Based on the author's experiences as an attorney and prosecutor for the state of Maine, this is a passionate and well-documented book about turning bias, prejudice, harassment, and violence among students into respectful interactions. The emphasis is on middle school and high school.

Schools Where Everyone Belongs: Practical Strategies for Reducing Bullying, 2nd edition, by Stan Davis, with Julia Davis, Research Press, 2007.

Stan Davis draws on theory and research to offer practical guidelines for implementing a whole-school approach to reducing bullying.

They Don't Like Me: Lessons on Bullying and Teasing from a Preschool Classroom by Jane Katch, Beacon Press, 2003.

Jane Katch has taught young children for many years. In this book, she reflects on a year of teaching four- and five-year-olds, with a particular focus on the children's social relations and power dynamics.

You Can't Say You Can't Play by Vivian Gussin Paley, Harvard University Press, 1992.

Author and teacher Vivian Paley spent a year investigating ways to help the kindergarten students she taught be more inclusive. She recorded her strategies, reflections, and results.

Websites

Cfchildren.org/programs/str/overview

The website for the Steps to Respect Bullying Prevention Program, developed by the Committee for Children, includes information about bullying, research, and services for schools.

Olweus.org

The website for the Olweus Bullying Prevention Program (program used by many schools in the U.S.) includes resources, research information, and information about services.

Opheliaproject.org

The website for the Ophelia Project includes resources, research information, and information about services focused on relational aggression.

Peacefulschoolbus.com

The website for the Peaceful School Bus program includes information about the schoolwide program for decreasing mean behavior on school buses and increasing respect and cooperation.

Stopbullying.gov

This federal government website is packed full of information for teachers, parents, and children.

Stopbullyingnow.com

The website of Stan Davis, author and consultant to schools about bullying prevention, includes his most current thinking about bullying and mean behavior and strategies for stopping mean behavior.

Child Development

Child Development Pamphlets: K–8, Northeast Foundation for Children, Inc., 2005.

Based on information in *Yardsticks*, these tri-fold brochures summarize common emotional, social, physical, and cognitive developmental characteristics of children in grades K–8. One brochure per grade, each covering the three ages typically seen at that grade level. Available in English and Spanish versions.

Yardsticks: Children in the Classroom Ages 4–14, 3rd edition, by Chip Wood, Northeast Foundation for Children, Inc., 2007.

This book offers clear descriptions of children's development and implications for the classroom, from age 4 to age 14.

Classroom Management

Closing Circles: 50 Activities for Ending the Day in a Positive Way by Dana Januszka and Kristen Vincent, Northeast Foundation for Children, Inc., 2012.

A collection of very brief (5- to 10-minute) activities that reaffirm classroom community, bring the day to a peaceful end, and let students and teachers alike leave school feeling encouraged and competent. Includes tips on finding time for closing circles.

Interactive Modeling: A Powerful Technique for Teaching Children by Margaret Berry Wilson, Northeast Foundation for Children, Inc., 2012.

Provides step-by-step guidance on use of the *Responsive Classroom* strategy of Interactive Modeling, including classroom examples, tips for use in different classroom situations, and scripts that teachers can follow.

What Every Teacher Needs to Know K–5 series by Mike Anderson and Margaret Berry Wilson, Northeast Foundation for Children, Inc., 2010 and 2011.

The series includes one book at each grade level. Includes information about common developmental characteristics as well as practical suggestions for arranging the classroom, scheduling the day, teaching routines, planning special projects, and communicating with parents.

Games and Movement Activities

85 Engaging Movement Activities by Phyllis Weikart and Elizabeth Carlton, HighScope Press, 2002.

Ideas for challenging and enjoyable movement experiences that develop academic and cooperative decision-making skills.

Energizers! 88 Quick Movement Activities That Refresh and Refocus, K–6 by Susan Lattanzi Roser, Northeast Foundation for Children, Inc., 2009.

Directions for quick movement activities that can be used in Morning Meeting, at transition times, whenever children need a movement break in the classroom, and on the playground.

The Incredible Indoor Games Book by Bob Gregson, McGraw-Hill, 2004.

177 group projects, games, and activities for indoor play.

36 Games Kids Love to Play by Adrian Harrison, Northeast Foundation for Children, Inc., 2002.

Clear, straightforward instructions for community-building, cooperative games that will maximize fun and minimize risk. Best for grades K–4.

Tried and True Classroom Games and Greetings by Origins, The Origins Program, 2010. Available from originsonline.org.

Directions for thirty games and twenty greetings that are favorites of teachers and students. Best for grades 4–9.

Morning Meeting

Books

Doing Math in Morning Meeting: 150 Quick Activities That Connect to Your Curriculum by Andy Dousis and Margaret Berry Wilson, Northeast Foundation for Children, Inc., 2010.

Ideas for math activities suitable for kindergartners to fifth graders and math-themed ideas for all four Morning Meeting components.

80 Morning Meeting Ideas for Grades K–2 by Susan Lattanzi Roser, Northeast Foundation for Children, Inc., 2012

80 Morning Meeting Ideas for Grades 3–6 by Carol Davis, Northeast Foundation for Children, Inc., 2012.

Twenty ideas for each component of Morning Meeting (greeting, sharing, group activity, and morning message) plus many tips for getting the most out of each idea.

The Morning Meeting Book by Roxann Kriete, with contributions by Lynn Bechtel, Northeast Foundation for Children, Inc., 2002.

In-depth information about each component of Morning Meeting plus appendices of greetings and group activities.

Morning Meeting Messages, K–6: 180 Sample Charts from Three Classrooms by Rosalea S. Fisher, Eric Henry, and Deborah Porter, Northeast Foundation for Children, Inc., 2006.

Includes sample charts at three grade levels, guidelines for creating charts, and suggestions for how to use the charts during Morning Meeting and throughout the day.

99 Activities and Greetings: Great for Morning Meeting . . . and other meetings, too! by Melissa Correa-Connolly, Northeast Foundation for Children, Inc., 2004.

Directions for greetings and activities for both primary and upper elementary grades.

DVDs

Morning Meeting Activities in a Responsive Classroom, DVD, Northeast Foundation for Children, Inc., 2008.

Morning Meeting group activities in action in K–3 classrooms.

Morning Meeting Greetings in a Responsive Classroom, DVD, Northeast Foundation for Children, Inc., 2008.

Morning Meeting greetings in action in K–5 classrooms.

Sample Morning Meetings in a Responsive Classroom, DVD and viewing guide, Northeast Foundation for Children, Inc., 2009.

Four complete Morning Meetings in K–3 classrooms.

Parent Communication

Parents and Teachers Working Together by Carol Davis and Alice Yang, Northeast Foundation for Children, Inc., 2005.

Comprehensive guide to building positive relationships with parents—includes information on working with diverse family cultures, setting the stage for a positive relationship during the early weeks of school, keeping in touch all year long, and helping parents understand classroom practices.

Problem-Solving Strategies

Sammy and His Behavior Problems: Stories and Strategies from a Teacher's Year by Caltha Crowe, Northeast Foundation for Children, Inc., 2010.

Tells the story of the author's work with a challenging student—includes practical strategies and reflection on both successes and challenges.

Solving Thorny Behavior Problems: How Teachers and Students Can Work Together by Caltha Crowe, Northeast Foundation for Children, Inc., 2009.

Presents five practical strategies that will help teachers and children solve common behavior problems together—includes information about problem-solving conferences, conflict resolution, role-playing, class meetings, and individual written agreements.

Rules and *Responsive Classroom* Approach to Discipline

Books

Rules in School: Teaching Discipline in the Responsive Classroom, 2nd edition, by Kathryn Brady, Mary Beth Forton, and Deborah Porter, Northeast Foundation for Children, Inc., 2011.

A comprehensive guide to the *Responsive Classroom* approach to classroom discipline; includes information and classroom examples for setting goals with students, creating rules collaboratively, using Interactive Modeling and role-playing to help children apply the rules to daily situations, and responding to misbehavior.

Teaching Children to Care: Classroom Management for Ethical and Academic Growth, K–8, revised edition, by Ruth Sidney Charney, Northeast Foundation for Children, Inc., 2002.

An in-depth look at classroom management; includes information about setting priorities and expectations with children, establishing classroom routines, generating rules with students, using logical consequences, planning and conducting social conferences and class meetings, and avoiding power struggles.

DVD

Creating Rules with Students, DVD, Northeast Foundation for Children, Inc., 2007.

Filmed in Caltha Crowe's third grade classroom in the early weeks of school—shows each step in the collaborative rule creation process.

Teacher Language

Book

The Power of Our Words: Teacher Language That Helps Children Learn by Paula Denton, EdD, Northeast Foundation for Children, Inc., 2007.

Provides an in-depth look at the *Responsive Classroom* approach to teacher language with a chapter each for use of envisioning language, open-ended questions, listening, reinforcing language, reminders, and redirections. Includes many examples of these kinds of language as used in classrooms.

DVD

Teacher Language in a Responsive Classroom, DVD, Northeast Foundation for Children, Inc., 2009.

Examples of teachers, grades K–4, using reinforcing, reminding, and redirecting language in classrooms and on the playground.

Alsaker, F. (n.d.). Bullying in Kindergarten. Retrieved February 2010 from www.education.com/reference/article/kindergarten-bullying/.

Astor, R., Meyer, H., & Pitner, R. (2001). Elementary and Middle School Students' Perceptions of Violence-Prone School Subcontexts. *Elementary School Journal, 101*, 511–528. As reported in Swearer, S., Espelage, D., & Napolitano, S. (2009). *Bullying Prevention and Intervention.* New York: Guilford Press.

Bear, G. G. (1998). School Discipline in the United States: Prevention, Correction, and Long-Term Social Development. *School Psychology Review, 1*(27), 14–32.

Bradshaw, C. P., Sawyer, A. L., & O'Brennan, L. M. (2007). Bullying and Peer Victimization at School: Perceptual Differences Between Students and School Staff. *School Psychology Review, 3*(36), 361–382.

Buhs, E., Ladd, G., & Herald-Brown, S. (2010). Victimization and Exclusion: Links to Peer Rejection, Classroom Engagement, and Achievement. In S. Jimerson, S. Swearer, & D. Espelage (Eds.), *Handbook of Bullying in Schools: An International Perspective* (pp. 163–172). New York: Routledge.

Bullock, J. (2002). Bullying Among Children. *Childhood Education, 3*(78), 130–133.

Card, N., & Hodges, E. (2008). Peer Victimization Among Schoolchildren: Correlations, Causes, Consequences, and Considerations in Assessment and Intervention. *School Psychology Quarterly, 4*(23), 451–461.

Coloroso, B. (2003). *The Bully, the Bullied, and the Bystander: From Preschool to High School—How Parents and Teachers Can Help Break the Cycle of Violence.* New York: Harper Collins.

Craig, W. M., & Pepler, D. J. (1998). Observations of Bullying and Victimization in the School Yard. *Canadian Journal of School Psychology, 13*(2), 41–59.

Davis, S., with Davis, J. (2007a). *Empowering Bystanders in Bullying Prevention*. Champaign, IL: Research Press.

Davis, S., with Davis, J. (2007b). *Schools Where Everyone Belongs: Practical Strategies for Reducing Bullying*. Wayne, ME: Stop Bullying Now.

Davis, S., & Nixon, C. (2010). The Youth Voice Project. Retrieved January 14, 2012, from www.stopbullyingnow.com.

Dillon, J. (2008). *The Peaceful School Bus Program—A Program for Grades K–12*. Center City, MN: Hazelden.

Englander, E. (2011, January 19). Presentation at the Bullying and Cyberbullying Prevention for Educators conference, Hampden-Wilbraham School District, MA.

Englander, E., & Schank, K. (2010, October 6). Reducing Bullying and Cyber Bullying: Ten Easy Tips for Educators Can Help Prevent Bullying in Schools and Online. Retrieved October 24, 2010, from www.eschoolnews.com/2010/10/06/reducing-bullying-and-cyberbullying/.

Farrington, D., & Ttofi, M. (2009). *School-Based Programs to Reduce Bullying and Victimization*. Campbell Systematic Reviews 2009:6. Retrieved from www.campbellcollaboration.org.

Faris, R., & Felmlee, D. (2011). Status Struggles, Network Centrality and Gender Segregation in Same- and Cross-Gender Aggression. *American Sociological Review, 1*(76), 48–73.

Felix, E. D., & Green, J. G. (2010). Popular Girls and Brawny Boys: The Role of Gender in Bullying and Victimization Experiences. In S. Jimerson, S. Swearer & D. Espelage (Eds.), *Handbook of Bullying in Schools: An International Perspective* (pp. 173–186). New York: Routledge.

Freiberg, J. (2009). *Confronting and Working to Reduce Bullying Behaviors in School Settings*. Medina, WA: Institute for Educational Development.

Gordon, S. (2010, May). Bullies Target Obese Kids. Retrieved May 2011 from http://health.usnews.com/health-news/family-health/brain-and-behavior/articles/2010/05/03/bullies-target-obese-kids.

Gottfredson, D. C. (2001). *Schools and Delinquency.* Cambridge, England: Cambridge University Press.

Greene, M. B. (2006). Bullying in Schools: A Plea for Measure of Human Rights. *Journal of Social Issues, 1*(62), 63–79.

Harachi, T., Fleming, C., White, H., Ensminger, M., Abbott, R., Catalano, R., & Haggerty, K. (2006). Aggressive Behavior Among Girls and Boys During Middle Childhood: Predictors and Sequelae of Trajectory Group Membership. *Aggressive Behavior, 4*(32), 279–293.

Henry, D., Guerra, N., Huesmann, R., Tolan, P., VanAcker, R., & Eron, L. (2000). Normative Influences on Aggression in Urban Elementary School Classrooms. *American Journal of Community Psychology, 1*(28), 59–81.

Hodges, E., Malone, M., & Perry, D. (1997). Individual Risk and Social Risk as Interacting Determinants of Victimization in the Peer Group. *Developmental Psychology, 33*: 1032–1039. As reported in Steps to Respect Review of Research, *Steps to Respect Program Guide*, Committee for Children, retrieved October 2010, from www.cfchildren.org/media/files/str_research_foundations.pdf.

Kasen, S., Berenson, K., Cohen, P., & Johnson, J. (2004). The Effects of School Climate on Changes in Aggressive and Other Behaviors Related to Bullying. In D. Espelage & S. Swearer (Eds.), *Bullying in American Schools: A Social-Ecological Perspective on Prevention and Intervention* (pp. 187–210). Mahwah, NJ: Lawrence Erlbaum Associates, Inc.

Katz, L., & Chard, S. (2000). *Engaging Children's Minds: The Project Approach.* Stamford, CT: Ablex Publishing Corporation.

Kaufman, J. (1994). Violence and Aggression of Children and Youth: A Call for Action. *Preventing School Failure: Alternative Education for Children and Youth, 3*(38), 8–9.

McCain, B., & Leonardo, T. (illus.). (2001). *Nobody Knew What to Do: A Story About Bullying.* Morton Grove, IL: Albert Whitman.

Menesini, E., Sanchez, V., Fonzi, A., Ortega, R., Constabile, A., & Lo Feudo, G. (2003). Moral Emotions and Bullying: A Cross-National Comparison of Differences Between Bullies, Victims, and Outsiders. *Aggressive Behavior, 6*(29), 515–530.

Moretsky, M., & Thomas, C. (2010). *Prevent Bullying in Elementary School with the STEPS TO RESPECT Program.* Retrieved September 30, 2010, from www.cfchildren.org/programs/free-webinars/channel/.

Newman, R. S., Murray, B., & Lussier, C. (2001). Confrontation with Aggressive Peers at School: Students' Reluctance to Seek Help from the Teacher. *Journal of Educational Psychology, 2*(93), 398–410.

Olweus, D. (1993). *Bullying at School: What We Know and What We Can Do.* Oxford, England: Blackwell Publishing Ltd.

Olweus, D., & Limber, S. (2010, October 20). *Bullying in the U.S.: Are We Making the Grade?* Retrieved October 20, 2010, from www.olweus.org/public/webinars.page.

Olweus, D., Limber, S., Flerx, V., Mullin, N., Riese, J., & Snyder, M. (2007). *Olweus Bullying Prevention Program Teacher Guide.* Center City, MN: Hazelden.

Olweus, D., Limber, S., & Mihalic, S. (2000). *Bullying Prevention Program: Blue Prints for Violence Prevention, Book Nine.* Blueprints for Violence Prevention Series. Boulder, CO: Center for the Study and Prevention of Violence, Institute of Behavioral Science, University of Colorado.

Orpinas, P., & Horne, A. (2010). Creating a Positive School Climate and Developing Social Competence. In S. Jimerson, S. Swearer, & D. Espelage (Eds.), *Handbook of Bullying in Schools: An International Perspective* (pp. 49–59). New York: Routledge.

Paley, V. G. (1992). *You Can't Say You Can't Play.* Cambridge, MA: Harvard University Press.

Parker-Roerden, L., Rudewick, D., & Gorton, D. (2007). *Direct from the Field: A Guide to Bullying Prevention.* Boston, MA: Commonwealth of Massachusetts, Department of Public Health.

Pellegrini, A. D., Long, J., Solberg, D., Roseth, C., Dupuis, D., Bohn, C., & Hickey, M. (2010). Bullying and Social Status During School Transitions. In Jimerson, S., Swearer, S., & Espelage, D. (Eds.), *Handbook of Bullying in Schools: An International Perspective* (pp. 199–210). New York: Routledge.

Pellegrini, A. D., Roseth, C., Mliner, S., Bohn, C., Van Ryzin, M., Vance, N., Cheatham, C. L., & Tarullo, A. (2007). Social Dominance in Preschool Classrooms. *Journal of Comparative Psychology, 1*(121), 54–64.

Pepler, D., & Craig, W. (2007) Binoculars on Bullying: A New Solution to Protect and Connect Children. Retrieved November 28, 2011, from www.canadiansafeschools.com/programs/research.htm.

Pepler, D., Craig, W., and O'Connell, P. (2010). Peer Processes in Bullying: Informing Prevention and Intervention Strategies. In S. Jimerson, S. Swearer, & D. Espelage (Eds.), *Handbook of Bullying in Schools: An International Perspective* (pp. 469–479). New York: Routledge.

Rigby, K., & Bauman, S. (2010). How School Personnel Tackle Cases of Bullying: A Critical Examination. In S. Jimerson, S. Swearer, & D. Espelage (Eds.), *Handbook of Bullying in Schools: An International Perspective* (pp. 455–468). New York: Routledge.

Rodkin, P. C., & Gest, S. D. (2011). Teaching Practices, Classroom Peer Ecologies, and Bullying Behaviors among Schoolchildren. In D. Espelage & S. Swearer (Eds.), *Bullying in North American Schools* (pp. 75–90). New York: Routledge.

Salmivalli, C., Kärnä, A., & Poskiparta, E. (2010). From Peer Putdowns to Peer Support: A Theoretical Model and How It Translated into a National Anti-Bullying Program. In S. Jimerson, S. Swearer, & D. Espelage (Eds.), *Handbook of Bullying in Schools: An International Perspective* (pp. 441–454). New York: Routledge.

Smith, P., Madsen, K., & Moody, J. (1999). What Causes the Age Decline in Reports of Being Bullied at School? *Educational Research, 3*(41), 267–285.

StopBullying.gov. (n.d.). *Myths About Bullying.* Retrieved December 12, 2011, from stopbullying.gov.

Swearer, S. (2010). *Risk Factors for and Outcomes of Bullying and Victimization.* Federal Bullying Prevention Summit. Retrieved October 2011 from stopbullying.gov.

Swearer, S., Espelage, D., & Napolitano, S. (2009). *Bullying Prevention and Intervention.* New York: Guilford Press.

Swearer, S., Espelage, D., Vaillancourt, T., & Hymel, S. (2010). What Can Be Done About School Bullying? Linking Research to Educational Practice. *Educational Researcher, 1*(39), 38–47.

Sweeting, H., & West, P. (2001). Being Different: Correlates of the Experience of Teasing and Bullying at Age 11. *Research Papers in Education: Policy and Practice, 3*(16), 225–246.

Vaillancourt, T., Hymel, S., & McDougall, P. (2003). Bullying Is Power: Implications for School-Based Intervention Strategies. *Journal of Applied School Psychology, 2*(19), 157–176.

Vygotsky, L. (1978). *Mind in Society.* Cambridge, MA: Harvard University Press.

Wessler, S. (2003). *The Respectful School: How Educators and Students Can Conquer Hate and Harassment.* With contributing author William Preble. Alexandria, VA: Association for Supervision and Curriculum Development.

Acknowledgments

This book reflects many people's thoughts and experiences. Scores of teachers, guidance counselors, administrators, and paraprofessionals invited me into their schools, classrooms, and work sites. They shared teaching materials and student-written reflections with me. They spent time telling me about their experiences with bullying and its prevention. They described student responses to bullying prevention practices that they've used in the past and practices that they are currently using. Without their help and input, this book would not have been possible. Among these educators are:

Stephanie Barry, Amy Bernard, Jessica Bessette, Cheryl Bliss, Sharon Brower, Sunday Burke, Ruth Burnett, Amy Calkins, Jessica Carey, Abby Clark, Bill Collins, Stacy Cope, Betsy Costello, Rosa DeVarona, Miguel DeJesus, Heather Robatille Dion, Stephanie Eleck, Kerri Falvo, Sarah Fillion, Soraya Gomes, Grace Halsey, Peter Halsey, Alycia Hause, Katherine Hayden, Christa Henderson, Linda Hudson, Donna Klaiber, Beth Krok, Cynthia Kruse, Jeff LaPlante, Angela Lariviere, Kathy Luchini, Connie Mahoney, Gail Manuel, Jodi McErlane, Tracy Mercier, Carrie Monachelli, Elizabeth Musgrave, Kimberly Myhre, Anne Nesbitt, Kathy Noler, Sheree Noley, Julie Nora, Judy Nuss, Jamie O'Hare, Lee Oldenberg, Susan Pelis, Jill Pszeniczny, Maureen Russell, Lori Saylor, Robyn Shuldman, Margaret Thompson, Eileen Tucker, Jamie Viesselman, Karen Wartel, Kevin White, Robin Whiteman, Chip Wood, Sherry Wood, and Ellen Zunick.

I learned such rich information from various workshops that I attended led by Stan Davis, Charisse Nixon, Jo Ann Freiberg, Marta Koonz, and Stephen Wessler. I appreciated Jo Ann's thoughts in conversations that we had while I was beginning to formulate my thinking about bullying. Her words, "If it's mean, intervene," echoed in my head every day and set the direction of my work. Stephen Wessler's descriptions of specific ways that disparaging words can escalate into violence guided my thinking from the early days of this project as well. Stan Davis's unique and thoughtful approach to bullying prevention has challenged my thinking and enriched my perspective throughout the writing of this book.

Not all workshops are in a physical site. The webinars offered by the Olweus Bullying Prevention Program and by the Committee for Children's program Steps to Respect were so helpful. I appreciate their generosity in offering them.

Chip Wood's comments on his blog have provided me with thought-provoking insights about children's social relationships since long before I began thinking specifically about bullying and continue to spark my thinking to this day.

Many people read and commented on the manuscript, bringing a wide range of perspectives to their reading. I would like to thank Jo Ann Freiberg, Stan Davis, Martha Hanley, Chris Carter, Jane Cofie-Raczko, Karen Casto, Richard Henning, Gretchen Bukowick, Carol Davis, Margaret Wilson, Tina Valentine, Alice Yang, and Mary Beth Forton.

Many people who work at Northeast Foundation for Children, home of the *Responsive Classroom* approach, reflected with me, suggested new ways of looking at bullying prevention, and helped me in ways too numerous to mention. Alice Yang and Mary Beth Forton saw the value in writing about bullying and enthusiastically encouraged me during the earliest phases of this project. For the past year and a half, Mike Anderson has sent me a flood of articles, web links, and emails full of information and ideas. Karen Casto has also offered information about bullying prevention, with a focus on schoolwide practice. Gail Lunetta has had the just-right example at the time when it's most needed. Tina Valentine has shared her experience from her career in elementary schools. Margaret Wilson has been there for me every step of the way. Whether she's helping to perfect a lesson, listening and responding to my musings, or giving me pointed feedback on my writing, Margaret has been an invaluable guide, mentor, and friend.

Lynn Bechtel, the editor and project manager for the book, has kept me on track with the correct turn of phrase, transition, and sentence construction as well as making sure that I've checked each and every fact. I appreciate her attention to detail. Elizabeth Nash brought her copyediting skills to the polishing of the manuscript and Cathy Hess was a meticulous proofreader. Helen Merena has, as always, designed a book that is both beautiful and useful.

My mother, Frances Crowe, has been a one-person cheering squad and a provider of articles and clippings both physical and electronic. My sister-in-law, Nancy Crowe, has been the source of rich and fruitful conversations. My daughter, Rosa Crowe-Allison, has been an enthusiastic partner in deep conversations, informed by her perspective as a psychologist. My life-partner, Jerry Allison, has provided feedback, hot meals while I worked, and fun every day, whether I'm sitting at home at the computer or out in the mountains with him.

Caltha Crowe's teaching career spanned thirty-eight years before she left the class-room in 2007. She taught a range of elementary grades and preschool in a variety of settings, including schools in urban New Haven, Connecticut, in the Chicago suburbs of Winnetka and Glencoe, and in Westport, Connecticut. During many of those years, Caltha was involved with Con-necticut's Beginning Educator Support and Training (BEST) program, serving as a mentor to new teachers, helping with mentor training, and serving on program advisory groups.

As a *Responsive Classroom*® consulting teacher, Caltha travels around the country to present workshops and coach teachers on using the *Responsive Classroom* approach. Caltha has a BA from Smith College, a master's degree in early childhood edu-cation from Goddard College, and a master's degree in educa-tional leadership from Bank Street College of Education.

About the Publisher

Publications and Resources

- Books, CDs, and DVDs for teachers and school leaders
- Professional development kits for school-based study
- Website with extensive library of free articles: www.responsiveclassroom.org
- Free quarterly newsletter for elementary educators
- The *Responsive®* blog, with news, ideas, and advice from and for elementary educators

Professional Development Services

- Introductory one-day workshops for teachers and administrators
- Week-long institutes offered nationwide each summer and on-site at schools
- Follow-up workshops and on-site consulting services to support implementation
- Development of teacher leaders to support schoolwide implementation
- Resources for site-based study
- National conference for administrators and teacher leaders

For details, contact:

Responsive Classroom®

Northeast Foundation for Children, Inc.
85 Avenue A, Suite 204, P.O. Box 718
Turners Falls, Massachusetts 01376-0718

800-360-6332 ■ www.responsiveclassroom.org
info@responsiveclassroom.org